# THE HUMAN IMPERATIVE

## ALEXANDER ALLAND, JR.

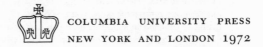

COLUMBIA UNIVERSITY PRESS
NEW YORK AND LONDON 1972

Alexander Alland, Jr., Associate Professor of Anthropology at Columbia University, is the author of *Adaptation in Cultural Evolution: An Approach to Medical Anthropology* (1970) and *Human Diversity* (1971).

COPYRIGHT © 1972 COLUMBIA UNIVERSITY PRESS
CLOTH-BOUND EDITION ISBN: 0-231-03228-5
PAPER-BOUND EDITION ISBN: 0-231-08301-7
LIBRARY OF CONGRESS CATALOG CARD NUMBER: 77-183227
PRINTED IN THE UNITED STATES OF AMERICA

FOR SONIA

# PREFACE

THE LAST FEW YEARS have seen a spate of books devoted to proving that human behavior is based either on instinct or on tightly controlled biological principles. Many of these have stressed instinctive aggression or territoriality as the key to an understanding of such social phenomena as war and property relations. Others have attempted to reduce human history to genetic principles or biologically locked sexual differences in behavior which keep men, but not women, in groups. A few have reintroduced racist arguments into scientific discourse. The major effect of these books has been to mislead or confuse those laymen who have little contact with scientific journals and little understanding of the complexities of recent work in such fields as behavioral genetics, ethology, physical anthropology, ethnology, sociology, and physiological psychology.

This book is offered both as a criticism of such overly simplistic approaches to human behavior and as a defense of Darwinian principles in both biology and the social sciences.

Between the writing of the first draft and the final manuscript this book has become something of a collective effort, although any errors which still cling to it are my own responsibility. I wish to thank in particular Elman R. Service, Marvin Harris, Abraham Rosman, Mimi Kaprow, Elizabeth Zinyei-Merse, Ralph Holloway, and Ben White. Special recognition goes to my wife Sonia whose most careful and critical reading of the manuscript in its various stages contributed greatly to the final product. I also owe a debt to my students, both undergraduate and graduate, at Columbia University, with whom pedagogy has, for me at least, been a two-way process.

Thanks are also due to the following publishers and individuals who granted permission to quote from previously published material: Holt, Rinehart and Winston Inc.; Doubleday and Company, Inc.; The American Psychological Association, publishers of *American Psychologist;* The American Geographical Society; Ashley Montagu; and Omer C. Stewart.

ALEXANDER ALLAND, JR.

*October, 1971*

# CONTENTS

# THE HUMAN IMPERATIVE

# CHAPTER 1

# INTRODUCTION

THIS BOOK IS A DEFENSE of man against strict biological determinism. A defense against those who, like Konrad Lorenz, Robert Ardrey, and Desmond Morris, would oversimplify man's place in nature and reduce human behavior to the level of instincts. The book is also a defense of anthropology against the claim that it is anti-Darwinian and unscientific. (Lorenz and Ardrey have created a pseudoconflict: science vs. romantic metaphysics.) They suggest that biologists see man as subject to laws of behavior, while social scientists see man as the subject of special creation and therefore immune to biological rules. This is not and has never been the case. The question is put too simplistically and the battle lines have been falsely drawn.

I am a Darwinian. The theory of evolution is the central focus of my thinking and research concerning human origins and behavior. I am also an anthropologist. My field is the science of man. This science, at least in the United States, has always maintained a dual focus: that of biology and of social science. Anthropologists have consistently held the point of view that, although man is a unique species, he can be understood only within the context of nature. This involves the study of human origins from primate ancestors, the emergence of man as a unique, culture-bearing species, and an understanding of the varied patterns of behavior which have been documented by ethnologists (those who study living societies around the world) throughout the past hundred years or so of modern anthropology.

This does not mean that anthropologists are biological determinists or that they follow a unified theoretical approach to the study of man. The premature publication of rather rigid social evolutionary theories in the late nineteenth century turned many anthropologists away from the idea that human behavior could be effectively placed in the Darwinian mold. Some of these theories obscured the useful aspects of evolutionary concepts because they argued from poorly constructed analogies rather than the main principles of modern Darwinism.

A renewed interest in the application of Darwinian biology to human behavior has developed in the last several years. This interest has opened an exciting field for theory and research specifically because it operates without the assumption that, since men are animals, they must behave like other animals. Instead, those interested in this approach search for both continuities and discontinuities in those processes which gave rise to man and which continue to influence his development.

Books like *African Genesis, The Territorial Imperative, On*

*Aggression,* and *The Naked Ape* (there are several more) obscure the real scientific progress that has been made in this area. These books oversimplify both Darwinism and the human condition. Their focus on hypothetical biological determinants of human social existence does not offer a plausible theory of human origins. Furthermore, these authors have been singularly unable to offer insights into the reasons for behavioral differences between groups, or to explain the complexities of human social patterns.

It is important to salvage those aspects of biological theory which can contribute to an understanding of man. The works named represent an intellectual dead end at a time when the complexities of human behavior can and must be probed in depth. The political and ecological situation in the world has reached a level of crisis approaching disaster. Outworn analyses such as those which equate war with innate aggression can only offer comfort to those who wish to maintain the *status quo.* Programmatic statements which call for instant population stability or phased decline only gloss over the serious problems of unequal production, distribution, and consumption. Static descriptions of human behavior which rest on incorrect or overly schematic analogies with lower animals and which deny historical process and evolution can only serve to blind us to the true problems facing mankind.

## EVOLUTION AND GENETICS

Darwin's theory of evolution is an elegant theory. With only a few basic assumptions it explains the development and diversification of life, and it is thus a major unifying concept in biology.

Darwin's major assumption was that all life is related, and

that the number of species occupying the earth has increased through time as a result of continual branching and development from ancestral forms. Evidence for this assumption has been accumulated by paleontologists whose investigations of the fossil record have provided a considerable body of information on the historical development of life on earth.

The theory proceeds to account for the process of diversification of living forms. Darwin (and Alfred Russel Wallace, the codiscoverer of the theory) suggested that the variation which exists in nature within and between species is, at least in a metaphorical sense, exploited by variations in the natural environment. Simply stated: where competition exists for such things as space or food, those organisms most fit to survive and reproduce in a particular environment will survive and reproduce in greater numbers than less well-adapted forms. If the process continues unabated for some time, less well-adapted forms will be reduced to insignificant numbers or be entirely eliminated from the population. Darwin called this process *natural selection*. In modern evolutionary theory the emphasis is on comparative reproduction rather than elimination because success is based on the genetic contribution made by an organism to the next generation.

The theory of evolution posits two sets of biological phenomena. One set provides relative stability in plant and animal species from generation to generation. Another set contributes some source of variation. The first are mechanisms of continuity, and the latter mechanisms of variation. While both sets are necessary for evolution, it is one of the paradoxes of biology that one, the mechanisms of continuity, reflects the perfection of biological systems and that the other, the mechanisms of variation, comprises nothing more than mistakes or errors in a process of replication. Without these mistakes there could be no evolution, and evolution, therefore, is in a very real sense an accidental process. What this means is that change does not occur in response to need. Nature does not provide species with the inherent ability to adapt to environmental variation. An evolutionary change can occur only if some variation already present within the population has a certain value as far as adaptation to new conditions is concerned. Once an adaptive trend has been established, however—that is, once a group of organisms has begun the shift toward a particular sort of adaptive change —this change will tend to continue in the same relative direction so long as there is adequate variation present and so long as the environmental demands remain relatively constant. If, for example, the development of an opposable thumb (the thumb opposite the fingers, as in the human hand) provides a group of tree-living animals with a distinct advantage for holding on, as opposed to falling, any variation in the direction of a better grasping hand will have a selective advantage. Thus a series of random or accidental events can under certain conditions lead to a predictable or nonrandom series of changes. If the environment selects only those forms which are best suited to prevailing conditions the possibilities for change are soon narrowed. As adjustment to a particular environment continues, the chances that widely divergent variations will survive decrease. Only those variations which represent improvement along the line of an established trend are likely to survive. Adaptation represents a goodness of fit between the form of the animal or plant species and the environment in which it must live. Another way of putting this is to say that a group of animals never invades a new environment fully adapted to it since adaptation involves interaction between the environment and certain biological characteristics of the organism. )

The mechanisms of variation and continuity can be fully understood only with the help of genetics, a science which was unknown in Darwin's time. The contribution of genetics to evolutionary theory lies in its detailed account of the sources of variation and continuity which occur within all living organisms. Combined with the study of environment and the fossil record, genetics helps us to understand not only what has occurred in evolution, but how and why it has happened. Let us examine the relationships between genetics and evolutionary theory.

First of all, consider some examples of continuity and variation as they appear in familiar situations.

It does not take an expert to predict that matings between purebred dogs will produce offspring very much like, but not exactly like, their parents. On the other hand, crosses between two different varieties of dog will produce offspring of greater variation and two mongrels of unknown origin will produce quite an unpredictable array of puppies. In all these cases, however, there is a considerable degree of continuity as well. All dogs produce dogs and not cats, and Great Danes produce dogs which are also Great Danes. Breeds, or subspecies, can be interbred to produce mongrels, but species generally cannot be crossed to produce intermediate varieties. In those few cases in which this rule is broken (tigers can breed with lions and horses with donkeys) the offspring are infertile. Thus the species is a closed unit. Members of a species can interbreed successfully, but they cannot produce fertile offspring if they breed with the members of some other species.

The source of much of the observed continuity is hereditary; that is, the reproductive process involves the transfer of
invariant genetic material from parent to offspring. Each
breed of dog, however, has thousands of units of genetic material which control such traits as size, shape, coat color,
length of tail, etc. In some cases a single unit controls a trait;
in other cases many units combine to produce a trait. Within
any species some of these genetic units are held in common
by all members of the species, while others are specific to
specific breeds. The distinctive attributes of dogs are the result of genetic units distributed throughout the species. The
distinctiveness of Great Danes is the result of units distributed within a single breed. Still other genetic units are restricted further in their distribution and account for individual differences within a breed. These units or genes are
generally passed on unchanged from parent to offspring, but
an offspring receives only one half of its genes from each parent. When two purebred dogs of the same strain mate, much
of the genetic material passed on to the offspring from each
parent is similar and little variation results. When mongrels
mate, the situation is somewhat different. Genes are passed
on unchanged to the offspring, but these genes themselves
represent a wider variety of traits because some represent one
breed, some another, some still another. These units combine
at random in the puppies, and greater variation results. It is
important to emphasize that the genetic units themselves do
not change from one generation to the next. It is only the
combination of these units which is different. The variation
which is observed is due to new combinations of the invariant genetic units.

Unfortunately, a further complication emerges when we examine variation more closely. A good deal of difference can

be produced among littermates by varying certain nonhereditary conditions, such as the amount and kind of food given to different dogs, or the amount of exercise allowed to each. When we vary these conditions we are changing the environment. Some animals may be brought up in one type of environment and some in another. Any variation which results from this type of manipulation is the result of environmental factors. It is sometimes difficult to sort out which differences are due to environment and which are due to heredity. One way of separating these two factors is based on the observation that environmental differences (variations acquired during the lifetime of the animal) are not passed down to the next generation. This is another way of saying that acquired characteristics are not inherited. Breeding experiments can reveal which traits are hereditary.

Any differences produced by environmental variation fall within definite limits, for, while the environment can strongly influence the development of an individual animal, it can never transform it into something which lies beyond the boundaries of its own heredity.

Development, then, is determined by a combination of relatively constant factors, which are part of the organism's own potential, and external conditions which make up the life experience of the organism. Thus every creature is a product of its own particular environmental history and a part of the genetic history of its ancestors.

## GENOTYPE AND PHENOTYPE

For purposes of analysis the genetic background must be separated from environmental effects. This can be done experimentally by raising organisms in the same environment (that is, holding environment constant) and noting the genetic variation; or by producing a pure strain of organisms with practically identical heredity, manipulating the environment, and noting its effect on variation. Purely genetic effects can also be analyzed by observing hereditary continuity from generation to generation in controlled breeding experiments. Technically the genetiĉ background of the organism, which can include a range of unexpressed traits, is called the *genotype*. The genotype represents the hereditary potential of an organism. Heredity (the genotype) acting in combination with a particular environment produces the *phenotype* or product of interaction. Another way of expressing this is to say that the phenotype is the result of a particular heredity acting on a particular environmental background. Any variation we observe among the members of a related group of organisms living under natural conditions must be phenotypic variation, because it will be the result of different environmental pressures and different genetic histories. Phenotypic variation in a population is the sum of genotypic variation inherent in the combined heredity of the group plus that part of environmental variation which affects the phenotype. This can be expressed in the formula $P_v = E_v + G_v$ in which $P_v =$ phenotypic variation, $E_v =$ environmental variation, and $G_v =$ genotypic variation.

From this formula one might surmise that a high degree of phenotypic variation in any given population will occur as the result of high genetic variation, high environmental variation, or a combination of the two.

Indeed this is often the case, but it must be noted that the genetic background itself can determine how much and what kind of environmental variation the phenotype can absorb. Some species are highly susceptible to environmental differences; others can remain stable under a wide range of conditions. Stability can result from two different genetic processes. In some species even small environmental variations are not well tolerated. If a population of such a species is exposed to changed conditions, it will die out. Many microorganisms (bacteria, for example) are so sensitive to such conditions as level of acidity or temperature that they will tolerate only minute differences. Such species will be found only where environmental variation is low, and the phenotypic variation will always be low as well. On the other hand, the genotypic background of other species may be geared to absorb a wide range of environmental variation without developing changes in the phenotype. Man, relatively speaking, is this type of organism.

It follows from evolutionary theory that environmental pressures act on all populations to select the best adapted phenotypes. If genotypic variation is submerged in a single phenotype, the variation itself can be preserved in the adaptive process. If, on the other hand, most genetic variation is expressed in variant phenotypes, genotypic variation is lowered. It must be made clear that in both situations the environment acts directly only on the phenotype, on what is expressed. Any effect on the genotype is indirect. This is of great importance in evolution, since the genotype can represent a reservoir of untapped variation which can be crucial to survival under critical conditions.

What I have been talking about in these last paragraphs is natural selection, for natural selection represents the effect of the environment on the phenotypes of a specific set of organisms, a population. Within the range of variation those organisms which are phenotypically best suited to the environment will have a selective advantage over the others.

While all organisms as individuals are the products of evolutionary development, evolutionary theory affords predictions about populations, and not about individuals. Statements made about natural selection are called statistical predictions because they involve probability and are never absolute. They can never give an investigator the assurance that a particular individual will survive. Such predictions represent a percentage figure based on the expected selection value for a specific trait or phenotype. Of course there are situations in which a trait is 100 percent fatal at or near birth. In these special cases it can be said with certainty that any organism born with such a trait will not live to reproduce itself. Its reproductive potential is said to be zero. This fact does not invalidate the rule that one cannot predict which organisms will live to reproduce, however! It should be obvious from the above that selective advantage is always a comparative figure. There is no such thing as an absolute selective advantage, because selection is measured by comparing the reproductive potential of one genotype against the reproductive potential of another genotype.

Statistical statements about survival value are always made in reference to a specific environmental background. The over-all picture of evolutionary development which has been so well analyzed by paleontologists and geneticists is made up of small pieces each representing a population, changing through time, each contributing in a small way to the over-all process of development. This is an extremely slow process, and it is therefore difficult to observe it in action. Genetic changes are minute, and a long time is usually required before their additive effects can be demonstrated. Some small but important adaptive changes have been documented, however, particularly in species which reproduce very rapidly

and which therefore can be studied through several generations by a single investigator in a reasonable length of time.

## SPECIATION

All these examples of variation have been contained within a
definite range of continuity, that of the species. I have dis-
cussed variations based on heredity and environment and the
process of natural selection through which these variations
are exploited, but I have also stressed that dogs remain dogs;
cats, cats; rabbits, rabbits. There appears to be some sort of
boundary to genetic variation, a boundary maintained by the
integrity of the species. This is because interbreeding between species does not normally produce fertile offspring,
hence genes cannot be spread through intermixture from one
species to another. How then can the Darwinian theory, even
with the help of genetics, explain the changes that must have
occurred across the dividing line between species? How can
the origin of species be explained from the principles dis-
cussed thus far? This is one of the most important questions
in evolutionary theory, and it is the one most frequently
asked by Darwin's critics, most of whom will admit that adaptation does indeed occur. Until *speciation,* the transformation from one species to another, is explained and until experimental evidence for its occurrence has been presented, they
refuse to admit any link between what they know to be true
about animal breeding and Darwin's theory. Essentially they
conceive of differences within species (for example, breed differences) as differences of degree, and differences between
species as differences of kind. By definition, species are reproductively isolated groups or closed units while breeds, or subspecies, of the same species are open units among which

breeding can occur. Reproductive isolation may be due to genetic or behavioral factors, but our main concern here will be with genetic factors (a full discussion of speciation can be found in Ernst Mayr's *Animal Species and Evolution*).

The demand for an explanation of speciation and evidence to support it is a just one. If evolutionary theory could not account for the transformation of species it would be useless, since this is its major task. Fortunately there are two solutions to the problem, two separate lines of evidence which demonstrate that speciation has occurred. One is historical and comes from the fossil record; the other is genetic and is found in the study of contemporaneous populations.

## FOSSILS AND SPECIATION

In the first place, the fossil record allows us to trace the sequential transformation of particular species. In the second place, it provides comparative material illustrative of branching evolution from parental forms. Sequential transformation and branching are both best explained as evolutionary adaptation to environment. In the first case (known as *anagenesis*) a single type develops greater and greater genetic specialization through time in areas where the environment has remained relatively constant. This is the progressive development of goodness of fit. In the second case (known as *cladogenesis*) related isolated populations differentiate from one another as a response to differential selection pressures which arise in different microenvironments. When these groups become reproductively isolated—that is, when they can no longer interbreed—the genetic differences between them have become great enough for them to fulfill the accepted definition of species.

Branching from common ancestors (cladogenesis), as well as progressive speciation (anagenesis), is documented by the record of the primate order, which includes man, monkeys, and apes. The common ancestors of these forms adapted more than seventy-five million years ago to life in the trees, in which stereoscopic vision and a pair of good grasping hands are advantageous. These are both major features of all but the oldest and most primitive members of the primate order. As the primates developed, they spread into different environmental zones. Some returned to a ground-dwelling existence and modified their earlier adaptations. Among these were the baboon and man, two species which have accommodated in different ways to terrestrial life. The human sequence shows increasing brain size, fully erect posture, and the loss of hands on the lower extremities.

In the last twenty years an impressively large group of fossils has been accumulated which help to fill in the details of man's evolution from earlier primate forms. This evidence would have been gratifying to Darwin. In his book *The Descent of Man* Darwin placed the human species among the other members of the animal kingdom and suggested that human evolution has followed the same rules set down in his earlier work, *The Origin of Species.*

The fossil record is useful not only because it allows us to examine a substantial part of a family tree through the course of its development, but also because it provides a good time sequence as well as some idea of the spatial distribution of forms. Geologists have expended much effort to create devices for measuring geological time, and they have been quite successful. These geological clocks help the paleontologist to date his fossil finds and to place them in orderly sequence.

In all the related fossil series it is assumed that genetic differences provided the basis for change. But we must remember that genetic changes are random events and are generally
of small quantitative significance. It is for this reason that
evolution requires a tremendous amount of time for change to
become readily apparent. The earth has been in existence,
however, for over four billion years, and life for over half that
time. Considering that man is a new species (something over
two million years old) two billion years are certainly long
enough for all of evolution to have taken place.

There is another lesson in the fossil record—one which
supports the contention that evolution based on genetic
change is an accidental random process. This is the fact that
in the time since the origin of life a tremendous number of
plants and animals have become extinct. Species have often
followed the "wrong path" in the maze of survival and arrived at a dead end. Environmental changes which were not
matched by the independent process of genetic change led to
the extinction of many species. The argument that evolution
is a directed process, guided by some greater wisdom, is contradicted by the existence of so many "mistakes" in the history of plant and animal development. Things look perfect
only to those who see what remains after a sometimes tremendously wasteful process of elimination has continued
through an almost unbelievable length of time. This can be
said to be the best of all possible biological worlds only in
the sense that what is is possible—as the end product of a
long interaction between internal genetic factors and external
environmental conditions. Only a goodness of fit between
these factors can yield survival and survival is always provi-
sional, dependent upon changing conditions. A simple shift in

the environment, such as the introduction of a new or foreign species, can so upset the balance and "good sense" of nature as to destroy a part of the natural environment.

## GENETICS AND SPECIATION

Some opponents of Darwin's theory do not accept the evidence of the fossil record. Among many poor criticisms they offer the more acceptable one that it is impossible to derive genetic data from bones. This is true, although Darwin's theory does not depend directly on genetics. Remember that Darwin wrote before there was a science of genetics. Darwin's theory with or without genetic evidence does explain quite satisfactorily what has been found in the paleontological sequences. Thus Darwinian evolution fulfills its scientific task by offering logical and empirically justifiable explanations for phenomena. But in addition there is genetic evidence for speciation—evidence which adds great weight to the paleontological record. This genetic evidence can best be explained by the examination of an abstract case.

Let us begin by assuming that a sexually reproducing, relatively homogeneous species lives within a small, restricted environmental zone. Let us further assume that this species constitutes a single breeding population. This means that any member of the population has an equally good chance to mate with any other mature member of that population that is of the opposite sex. Such a situation would ensure a wide and random distribution of genes in the population at large. Random mating of this type is known as *panmixis*. When it occurs the population is said to share a common *gene pool*. Any variation which exists in such a population will be distributed fairly evenly within the confines of the total group.

Now if this is a particularly successful species and it spreads out geographically, it is likely that subpopulations will develop as units of the larger group. If the distance between these groups widens, they will eventually constitute separate breeding groups. This is largely a mechanical situation. Animals which are closer together are more likely to breed with each other than animals which are far apart. If any barriers develop between units, these units will become at least partially isolated. In such situations new genetic variations will be unequally distributed in the species at large. That is, each subgroup will begin to develop its own gene pool different in some respects from all other gene pools. If the geographic space in which the species is distributed is uneven—that is, if there are environmental variations to which the species is sensitive—different selection pressures will further differentiate the gene pools of the subgroups. As long as some interbreeding continues to occur between these subpopulations, there will be no differentiation beyond the level of the species. Each individual unit will constitute a separate breed or strain of the species. If, however, for some reason some of the populations become totally isolated, they will continue to change to the point where genetic differences will be great enough to produce new species. As I have pointed out above, the reason most species cannot interbreed successfully is that they are rather radically distinct units, units between which there is a sizable amount of genetic difference. As long as gene flow continues, enough genetic similarity will be preserved between strains to stop the process of speciation from reaching finality. Under natural conditions subpopulations tend to become separated through such centrifugal processes as differential genetic variation, differential selection pressures, and semi-isolation, but they are also frequently drawn together by the centripetal process of gene flow. Speciation occurs when the centripetal forces are interrupted.

As far as speciation is concerned, then, we have evidence of developmental adaptation (anagenesis) and evidence of branching adaptation (cladogenesis) from the fossil record. Additional evidence from genetic studies of living populations supports the branching hypothesis of speciation. The arguments against Darwin's *Origin of Species* fall under attack from two independent sources of scientific evidence. Both sources point to the same phenomena, adaptation and differentiation through genetic mechanisms, acting in combination with environmental pressures. Speciation is a product of evolution in which variation is exploited to produce adaptation. When this variation develops in related populations which are isolated from one another, they become distinct units. As long as there is some gene flow between these units, a specific continuity will be maintained. As long as the environment is stable, this continuity will be reinforced by the fact that only certain genetic combinations will prove adaptive under specific conditions. When the environment varies beyond certain limits, the phenotypic variation inherent to some degree in all populations will either readjust to the new conditions or die out. Extinction results when none of the inherent genetic variation fits the new environmental demands.

Behavioral traits as well as physical traits have evolved. Even simple organisms such as protozoa (one-celled animals) respond automatically to certain stimuli such as light or acidity. Evolution has seen two major and interlocked trends in the development of behavior. These are automatic responses and learning. Most organisms display both types of behavior, and in many cases specific types of response reflect a combination of the two. Web spinning in spiders is automatic and occurs in response to internal stimuli as well as stimuli in the environmental field. Territorial and aggressive behavior, often of a highly patterned sort, also may occur in a wide variety of species. Such behavior when it occurs is stereotypic. That is, given certain conditions, one can predict exactly what the animal will do. Other behavior, which to the untrained eye may appear to be completely automatic, may result from learning which can take place only during a specific period in the development of the organism. Newly hatched ducklings, for example, will follow any sound-emitting moving object to which they are exposed. The response, however, will occur only within a brief time span after hatching. Under natural conditions the initial stimulus for a baby duck is its mother and so a naïve observer might assume that mother-following is an automatic unmodifiable response in ducks. Certain birds which appear to emit a mating call as an automatic response actually learn the call from other birds, but again only within a specific time period. The period of learning in which such behavior can be learned is coded genetically but not the actual learning itself.

In many cases the behavioral repertoire of an adult animal is the result of shaping a combination of a genetic potential and experience. This is not surprising. If phenotypic *physical* traits are a product of both genetic constitution and environmental history, why should phenotypic *behavioral* traits be otherwise? Nature and nurture play their role in both cases.

Automatic responses of a complex sort, such as nest building or mating behavior, have been labeled *instinctual* by many authors. For some (Lorenz in particular), an instinct is an hereditary invariable response which will be released sooner or later even in the absence of some appropriate outside stimuli or cue. For these authors, instincts are as much a part of anatomy as legs or eyes; they are destined to be expressed. For other authors (particularly Tinbergen), an instinct is an automatic (unlearned) response which is released in the presence of an appropriate stimuli. *Drives* (to borrow a term from psychology) are states in which an organism is irritated by some internal stimulus (often released by some external cue) to perform a behavior which satisfies the drive state. Hunger is such a drive. For many authors the difference between drives and instincts is that the response to a drive is not so rigidly patterned as the response to an instinct. The fact that man has a hunger drive, for example, really tells us nothing about how he will get his food or what he will eat. Both are patterned by learning and tradition. Items which would disgust some individuals are perfectly palatable to others. Think, for example, of cannibalism.

Few would deny that something like drives exists in man. What *is* usually argued is *what* drives are specific to man. Hunger, thirst, sex, and the need for sleep appear to be acceptable to everyone. More in doubt are drives for power, territory, aggression, and creativity.

Here I should like to introduce a distinction between a drive, which is deterministic only in a very loose sense, and capacity for behavior, which is even less deterministic. I would say that humans are born with capacities for aggression, territoriality, creativity, as well as many other types of behavior. The occurrence or nonoccurrence of such behavior in any individual or in any group, however, will depend upon a combination of hereditary factors and learning. The form that such behavior would take will also be patterned by the culture in which an individual is socialized.

If human beings in general have a capacity for aggressive behavior, they also have a capacity for tightrope walking and outcome of heredity and experience will lead to differences in temperament and ability which make it possible for the human group to function as a social entity.

The human being has been shaped by evolution. His size, the fact that he walks on two feet, his relative lack of body hair, and the fact that he can and does talk are all products of the evolutionary process. What man does and also what he believes are also products of evolution. *But* those elements which depend upon culture are not inherited biologically. In part, man adapts biologically to his environment in a non-biological way—through culture.

Since man is one of the most widely distributed of species occupying a vast array of environments ranging from deserts to swampland, from plains to mountains, from inland to the sea, and because his social and technological environment varies as widely, we should not be surprised to find a range of behavioral variation adjusted to specific environments.

The process of cultural adaptation can proceed on both the conscious and unconscious level. At the present time we are becoming aware of the dangers to life inherent in some of the technological practices we took for granted during the development of our modern industrial system. Recently air pollution and environmental wastage have become major problems. We have become conscious that our survival in a strictly biological sense depends upon a reevaluation of our use of natural resources and the development of long-range planning for environmental control and conservation.

Even small variations in the environment can affect the life chances of individuals and groups. These variations can operate on feelings of comfort and discomfort subliminally. People may then change their behavior unconsciously in order to ac-

juggling. (How good a circus performer one might be
probably a function of inborn ability, motivation, and
folding of ability through arduous training.) If this
case, I think one can see how vapid the concept of agg
becomes when an anthropologist attempts to say som
important about the social behavior of a specific group.
ing is automatic about such behavior. In fact, the onl
dences of specific automatic behavior in man are simp
flexes such as the knee jerk; the more complex response
infant to pressure on the cheek, which causes it to tu
ward the stimulus and begin sucking; and the (perhaj
stinctual) fear of falling which a baby expresses.

Anthropologists realized long ago that purely biologic;
planations of human behavior are inadequate. Our beh;
is based on customs which develop in the context of sp{
social and environmental conditions. While they do re
the fact that man like all other animals must adjust to the
vironment to survive, attempts to link human behavioral
tems to simple geographic or genetic factors have alv
failed. This is because man's major behavioral adaptatio
culture.

Culture is learned and shared. It is rooted in biology. I
although this is true (the capacity for culture is part of a n
mal human's brain structure), culture frees man to an unpr
edented degree from strictly biological controls over the (
velopment and maintenance of behavioral systems. Culture
biologically adaptive. That is, human populations imbedde
like all animal populations, in specific environments adjust
these environments largely through culture.

Man is born with a capacity to learn culture, not with cu
ture. This does not mean that all human behavior is freed (
biological programming. Individuals are born different. Th

commodate to minor changes in environmental information. This is also adaptation.

Humans, as members of social groups, may exhibit behaviors which parallel instinctual behaviors in lower animals, but which have their origin in culture. Variations, cultural or biological, are all subject to selection through the action of the environment. If a variation (physical or behavioral, genetic or learned) has an advantage over other existing forms in a specific environment, it can be selected for in that environment.

Behavioral adaptation can occur among groups vying for the same space. Those populations with more adaptive systems will have better survival chances than those with poorer systems. Thus groups with efficient means of waging war will have an advantage over other populations. Populations with more efficient social organization or production may also prove to be better adapted. Note also that if the criteria for evolution and adaptation involve selective fertility rather than selective mortality (the old survival of the fittest) those groups which for whatever reason reproduce and sustain themselves at a faster rate than other groups will come to replace the less efficient groups through time.

In short, culture, which is a product of man's biological past, and which is man's major way of adapting, is not dependent upon genetic variation for change. Aggressive or passive behavior (and combinations of these) are both possibilities within the behavioral capacities of man. What kind of behavioral system emerges must conform to man's biological capacities, but since these are wide, the capacities alone tell us little about real systems undergoing the selective process.

Certain conditions should produce parallels between behaviors such as territoriality in lower animals which are genetic in origin and culturally produced behaviors in man. In both cases the environment has favored behavior of a certain type, but in the first case the emergent form is directly under the control of biological mechanisms. In the latter case the adaptive behavior is selected from a wide range of possible behaviors none of which are specifically controlled by the genetic system.

Thus I am not surprised when I find territorial behavior in many human groups. Nor am I surprised to find aggressive behavior affecting various levels of that complex whole which makes up human social life. It is no surprise either that the anthropological record contains many cases of opposite types of behavior. No one type reflects the "real" innate nature of man. Human nature is largely open, and it is this very openness that gives the human species its great advantage in the biological world.

# CHAPTER 2

# AFRICAN GENESIS,
# EXODUS,
# LEVITICUS

THE COUNTERATTACK upon the assumed dictum of social science that the proper study of mankind is man alone has been led in the professional world by Konrad Lorenz. Lorenz, however, as we shall see later, attempts to draw a synthesis between the biological heritage in human behavior and its expression in culture. Robert Ardrey hews to a much stricter biological line. According to Ardrey, if we understand man's biology we understand human behavior in all its facets. Emphasis is placed on aggression, which Ardrey believes operates to insure an even more fundamental instinct in man: territoriality. Ardrey is so convinced of the primacy of territoriality over all other drives that he asks the question:

"How many men have you known of in your lifetime, who
died for their country? And how many for a female?" (*Territorial Imperative,* p. 6)

This sets the tone for a dramatic attempt to overwhelm the
reader. A moment's reflection must bring one to ponder those
social factors which take young men far from their own land
to die for causes only some of them understand and in which
only some of them are emotionally involved. Surely some die
for their country, some die for an ideology, and some die because they are impotent in the face of a system which sends
them to war. It is certainly easier to fight than to rebel
against authority.

Melodrama is not, however, Ardrey's only technique. His
argument often begins with sound scientific data and then
switches to a string of *non sequiturs* which are likely to mislead or confuse the lay reader. To maintain his argument he
makes it appear as if the experts are firmly in his camp. They
and he represent truth in a battle waged against a set of scientific nitwits who have been agents in a conspiracy to rob
the layman of access to scientific facts. This attitude is reinforced by his reliance upon the reverse *ad hominem* in which
the reader is warned that Ardrey will be attacked by liberals,
Marxists, and Freudians. The conspiratorial theory of history
is called forth as we are told that ameliatory social scientists
attracted to the classless state have forgotten "that hierarchy
is an institution of all social animals and the drive to dominate one's fellows an instinct three or four million years old."
(*African Genesis,* p. 13)

Similarly, "no child of ours . . . can differ at birth in significant measure from the earliest of *Homo-sapiens.* No instinct, whether physiological or cultural, that constituted a
part of the original human bundle can ever in the history of

the species be permanently suppressed or abandoned." Besides the fact that the term *cultural instinct* is a contradiction in itself, this statement is complete nonsense, for it reflects a dismal unawareness of the process of genetics in which the penetrance of a particular gene (the degree of its expression) is the complicated outcome of environmental and genetic processes. Genes are suppressed or modified by other genes in the genetic system and by the effects of environment on the maturing system.

It would seem as if science itself were driven by instinct. "The contemporary revolution in the natural sciences, unorganized, undirected, and largely unrecorded, has with a strong instinct for survival challenged the romantic fallacy in a voice unlikely to be heard." (*African Genesis*, p. 16) The enemy is clear, the political bias becomes clear also when we read that independence movements in Africa are reducing the continent to something approaching a political state of nature. (*African Genesis*, p. 22) This theme is further elaborated in *The Territorial Imperative* and we shall return to it below.

For Ardrey the naïve social scientist has been the victim of the so-called romantic fallacy. This fallacy is the belief that man is born good and that the evil which emanates from human behavior is due to the effects of the social environment. Following the fallacy, all one need to do to reach utopia is modify the environment and man's basic goodness (his primitive human nature) will emerge. This is a peculiar analysis, standing as a mere parody of Freud and Marx, as well as recent social science. Even the most behavioristically inclined psychologists and sociologists have been anything but romantic about man. They do not see man or any other species, for that matter, as good or evil, but rather as neither good nor evil. For what can "good" or "bad" mean, anyway, unless they are defined by men in the context of socially derived ethics? In fact, most behaviorists have been careful to avoid value terms in their theories, which are based upon operational concepts and empirical observation. This is not to say that early behaviorists did not place too much emphasis on environment in the process of development. But modern behaviorism as expressed in the work of behavior genetics and physiological psychology takes the sophisticated view that any behavioral output is the product of a complex process in which different genetic systems interact with different environments. Thus a *phenotype* (the outcome of individual chemistry and individual encounters with the environment) is not to be explained on the basis of a *genotype* (the hereditary information) alone.

Ardrey and Lorenz are content to substitute one doctrine for another. The one they choose is Original Sin. While Ardrey never expresses this overtly, Lorenz makes an explicit statement: "All the great dangers threatening humanity with extinction are direct consequences of conceptual thought and verbal speech. They drove man out of the paradise in which he could follow his instincts with impunity and do or not do whatever he pleased." (*On Aggression*, p. 29)

Ardrey begins substantively with a controversy concerning the remains of the Australopithecinae or South African Man Apes. These fossils, found originally in South Africa and now represented by specimens from East Africa and Ethiopia as well as other parts of the Old World, were originally taken to be man's near cousins, one of a possible series of dead ends in the process of human evolution. The chief argument against placing them in the main line of evolution was an initial lack of associated cultural evidence. In addition, the original dating of these fossils in the early pleistocene (less than one mil-

lion years ago) would have put them too late on the evolutionary scale to be antecedent to man. It is extremely difficult
to date hominid fossil material from South Africa because of
the rather undifferentiated geological strata. When the first
specimens of these ape-men or man-apes were found, none of
the modern chemical dating methods existed. Since that time
sophisticated techniques have been developed and we know
now that some Australopithecinae date as far back as three
million years. In addition, evidence has accumulated which
strongly supports the hypothesis that these creatures did
*make* and use tools of a particular style. This is important because such tool manufacture is accepted as the diagnostic for
man. (We now have evidence that chimpanzees also manufacture a crude tool which they use to extract termites from
their nests. This does not negate the definition, however. The
tool-making capabilities of the Australopithecinae are more
sophisticated than that of chimps and reflect a series of anatomical changes unknown in any living primate other than
man.)

Ardrey draws upon a dead argument to heighten the drama
of his own theory that man was, and still is, a killer. In this
he is aided by the speculations of the anatomist Raymond A.
Dart, who was among the first to suggest that tools, specifically for hunting, were used by the Australopithecinae. Before
recent discoveries the only evidence of tools among these fossil types was a rather ambiguous set of bones found in association with australopithecine skeletal material. The burden
of proof lay on Dart, who argued eloquently in favor of his
hypothesis. For some years his theory was countered by the
physical anthropologist Sherwood Washburn, and others who
felt that the evidence pointed to the opposite conclusion: that
these small primates were the hunted rather than the hunters.

The discovery of worked stone tools in East Africa put an end to this speculation. But Dart and Ardrey went beyond the evidence to suggest that because these creatures used tools some of which functioned as weapons, the tools were the artifacts of an aggressive species. Analysis of these crude chipped stones and bones suggests that they were used for a variety of purposes, among them hunting, but aggression and hunting cannot be equated.

There is much evidence and persuasive theory behind the idea that the transition from ape to man involved a change in diet from one based largely upon vegetable products to one based largely on meat. But when men, or other animals for that matter (with the possible exception of wolverines, minks, and weasels), kill animals of another species they do so for food. They kill in a predatory rather than an aggressive manner. The distinction between aggression and predation is important, for in aggression hostility is intraspecific while in predation killing, which need not be aggressive, is interspecific. There are many species, particularly among herbivors, which are aggressive, but nonpredatory. There are also predatory species which display little if any intraspecific aggression. Among human beings one of the most pacific cultural groups known, the pygmies of the Ituri forest, so well described by Colin Turnbull in his book *The Forest People,* are extremely adept hunters. Predators, yes, but aggressors, certainly not!

It is true also that man is one of the rare cannibalistic species, but this practice cannot be instinctual. For, if it were, cannibalism would certainly be more widely distributed than it is. A study of its distribution done several years ago by Robert K. Dentan showed that it tends to occur in protein scarce areas, and then only in combination with certain cultural facts which free men to eat conspecifics.

The pygmy case tells us that men who hunt will not necessarily kill other men. Nonetheless, the existence of such intraspecific killing as homicide, infanticide, gerontocide,
capital punishment, war, and sacrifice demands explanation.
To understand them as cultural phenomena, which indeed
they are, we must not lump them under a single heading. The
first four, for example, involve ingroup killing, war occurs between members of different groups, and sacrificial victims
may be chosen according to custom among one's own people
or among outsiders. Each type of killing has its own set of
causes rooted in social life and can be understood only in the
context of historical process.

For Ardrey the "weapon" has fathered the man. The
counter argument put forth by most physical anthropologists
is much more sophisticated and much more interesting. It is
also more in agreement with Darwin's theory of evolution as
it is now interpreted in modern biology. While Ardrey emphasizes competition between groups which can be summa-
rized in the cliché "survival of the fittest," modern biology
has come to recognize that selective fertility, that is, the production and survival of offspring, is the real key to evolution.
Evolutionary change occurs when one group out-reproduces
another or when individuals in one population out-reproduce
other members of that population. Reproductive efficiency is
dependent upon a wide range of biological and, in the case of
man, cultural factors.

Among modern anthropologists Sherwood Washburn has
been in the forefront of those who have suggested a relationship between tools (not just weapons) and the rapid evolution of the human species. The argument goes as follows: tool
use presented an immediate advantage for a rather weak species in its food quest. Any development in the direction of
improved tool manufacture and use would produce a con-

comitant advantage for those so endowed. Tool use, however, requires a certain type of physical structure the most important element of which is upright posture. Washburn suggested therefore that the first advance towards *Homo sapiens* was the development of true bipedalism which freed the hand for carrying and tool use. The intelligent use of tools, however, requires special cerebral organization producing higher intelligence and good eye–hand coordination. Better tools in combination with a cooperative social organization favor individuals with better brains, and better brains produce more complex and more adaptive tools. Communication systems, and eventually language, develop as a side effect of this process. Language of course is the *sine qua non* of human social organization. The rapid change in the morphological structure of fossil hominids which begins with upright posture and an anatomy adjusted to walking erect finishes with the development of bigger and also reorganized brains. The use of tools for hunting increases the calorie-getting efficiency of the group and allows for an expanded population. Even if differentially endowed groups of man-apes never met, and never fought a battle of "survival," those with more efficient hunting methods including both the tool–weapon and better social organization, as well as fuller knowledge of terrain and wildlife conditions would in time come to replace their dim-witted cousins. This would occur through the process of differential reproduction.

Furthermore, a more efficient technology would be capable of supporting a greater population. Since hunting as a way of life imposes rather strict upper limits on group size, however, successful groups would divide frequently, sending colonists outward to exploit new territories. Thus superior populations would not only increase in number but they would spread faster into empty territory. Differences between local environments would tend to stimulate new *culturally* based adaptations, although at a very primitive level of technological development extreme environmental differences would tend to set absolute geographic limits beyond which groups would be unable to spread. Population density at this early stage of development would probably be low, and hostile encounters between separate groups of ape-men would probably be rare. Later, when language developed, contiguous groups may well have had friendly relations since they must have been united through kinship bonds due both to the hiving off process and the forming of new alliances, through intergroup marriage.

Unlike Lorenz, who makes a clear distinction between aggression and predation, Ardrey assumes that the subsistence needs of the australopithecinae, that is, a dependence upon hunting, placed great selective advantage upon an aggressive instinct. Yet the social aspect of early human life must have fostered group cohesion, a process in which aggression against one's fellows would have to be modified. Ardrey counters this by saying that the aggressive instinct found its outlet in intergroup hostility, which in turn served to provide an outlet for the instinct and at the same time helped to forge the social bond within the group. But, as I have already stated, it is likely that intergroup aggression was of only slight importance in the life of early man. It was therefore unlikely to exert any strong selection pressures upon development.

In chapter 2 of *African Genesis,* Ardrey slips into his territorial thesis, which is developed in greater detail in *The Territorial Imperative*. Ardrey overstates his case at the outset. "When we find a characteristic prevalent among all branches of the vertebrates, such as the instinct to maintain and defend a territory, then we must mark it a significant instinct indeed." (*African Genesis,* p. 71) "Every primate species so far studied with the significant exception of the gorilla maintains and defends territories." (*African Genesis,* p. 72)

Among man's closest relatives (the simian apes: gorilla, chimpanzee, orang, and the gibbon) only the gibbon is clearly territorial and aggressive. Recent studies show that the gorilla is not the only rather shy nonterritorial animal but that this is true of the chimp and the orang as well. Ardrey, however, has a ready answer for this contradiction. The gorilla, he tells us, is an unsuccessful species on the threshold of extinction. Actually these animals were about as well adjusted to their environment for the past ten million years or so as any other primate species. Their immanent doom is the result of competition between themselves and man, and no species of vertebrate, no matter how territorial or aggressive, can compete with humans and survive. The great cats of the African plains, along with several species of ungulates, face the same problem as their primate cousins. In fact, unendangered species are those which either do not compete with man or which have been domesticated for human exploitation. Domestication generally has produced relatively passive nonaggressive animals except those used in hunting or guard work.

Allison Jolly, a zoologist who has published an extensive field study of lemur behavior, has this to say about aggression in the primate order:

> The level of aggression and the means of controlling it vary enormously among primates. Some genera of each branch seem to have suppressed the expression of aggression within a troop almost entirely—the howlers, the gorillas. In others—

particularly baboons, and macaques—aggressive interactions may be common. *Aggression among the same species in different environments also varies immensely* [italics mine]. Baboons and vervets in lush Ugandan forests may have far fewer aggressive interactions than those of the Tanganyikan plains. Macaque species may bite and wound while fighting, but Washburn and DeVore stress that baboons have checks and restraints: their frequent expressions of power and antagonism were only once seen to lead to injury. As Andrew has said, an animal with as much latent aggression as the baboon is under great selective pressure to maintain elaborate and exact means of communication to avoid real fights. (*Lemur Behavior,* p. 154)

Within the lemur pattern, as in other primates, the total level of aggression differs between genera. The placid *P. verreauxi* practically never dispute, while *L. catta* even at the calmest seasons will have several minor spats an hour. In both species, however, these mild disputes over precedence on a branch, or the right to groom an infant are of such low intensity they could hardly threaten the structure or cohesion of the group. These two genera recall differences between howlers and *Cebus* in the Panama forest, *Colobus* and baboons in Uganda, even langurs and macaques in India. It is apparently common for species which share the same trees to have widely different levels of aggression. (*Ibid.,* p. 155)

Thus, even in these primates where aggression appears to be a latent force its expression varies tremendously. The variance appears to be due to genetic differences and environmental structuring as well. In terms of modern genetic theory the probability that certain behaviors will occur is dependent not only upon a genetic substratum, but upon the modification, sometimes intense, that this structure undergoes in the interaction between biological heritage and environmental experience.

Ardrey and Lorenz both cite evidence to support the contention that the aggressive instinct serves to maintain the territorial integrity of social units and a dominance hierarchy within such units. The result of ingroup aggression, which generally takes a symbolic form, is to create a social order within the troop. This maintains stability and reduces overt hostile behavior which would otherwise lead to disorganization and death for some members of the community. This argument is certainly far removed from the initial one which states that it is man's killer instinct which provides the basis of human behavior. Ardrey, however, cannot resist the dramatic phrase. The murderous aspect of early man makes better copy than the development of social cohesion through cooperation, and a reduction in aggressive potential. Ardrey uses the word "assault" to refer to the hunting behavior of the Australopithecinae. He tells us that the "weapon is the hallmark of human culture" and he refers to man as the "weapon maker." It would be much more appropriate to refer to man as the symbol maker, for linguistic communication is the true hallmark of the human species. And it is the symbolic process which allows man to first think of and then create tools, among them weapons. But Ardrey goes even farther. He invents an instinct for weapons. "The acquisition of an instinct for weapons, if it existed, is simply an incident in the long story of human behavior." (*African Genesis*, p. 209)

Again Ardrey tells us: "Man is a predator whose natural instinct is to kill with a weapon." The question is to kill *what* with a weapon? And how could this "instinct" to kill with a weapon have arisen? Could it have been that the first man felt an unquenchable urge to seek out a weapon, and then a victim? Is this the aggressión which Ardrey and Lorenz admit is a relatively passive phenomenon? Lorenz has an an-

swer for this paradox by suggesting that man's ability to kill
has outstripped the biological restraints built into the aggressive response, but nowhere does he suggest that man has an
instinct to kill or an instinct to kill with weapons.

Washburn and DeVore, on the other hand, have suggested
that the large canines of male baboons are, at least in part, a
response to predator pressure. It is the large dominant males
who are responsible for the protection of the entire troop
from such natural enemies as panthers and hyenas. Thus,
such weapons are in large measure defensive rather than aggressive and directed against other species. If they also serve
as symbolic markers of dominance within the troop, so much
the better, but the selective pressures which favor them may
not be based on the preservation of an aggressive drive. I
would go further than Washburn and DeVore, for I do not
think that one can fully explain the evolution of land-dwell-
ing primate morphology, particularly human morphology, on
the basis of predator pressure alone. Washburn and DeVore
believe the long tooth can give way only with the development of a substitute, the tool (not necessarily a weapon, for
the teeth function in eating as well as killing, and the tool is
an aid in cutting and preparing meat, as well as a means of
killing game). As I hope to show below, other forces may
have played an important role in the evolution of human
physical and social structure.

Ardrey is wrong when he says that all primates (except go-
rillas) have instincts which demand maintenance and defense
of territories and that the formation of social bands is the
principal means of survival for physically vulnerable creatures. When he adds that amity and loyalty to social partners
and a universal system of dominance are the mechanisms
which provide for effective social life and elimination of the

weak he provides us with a combined picture which fits some primates but not others. It can be argued that the development of a dominance hierarchy serves to protect the weak as well as the most fit, unless the unfit are prevented in some way from mating. Primate studies demonstrate that low status males in some species do in fact have less chance of inseminating females, but in other species their chances are just about as good as any. Furthermore, the determination of low status in some species may be based not so much upon inherited physical characteristics as upon social characteristics. It has been found that the rank of an animal may be partially dependent upon the rank of its parent in the previous generation's social order!

It must be noted that any exceptions to Ardrey's collection of "biological facts" destroys his argument because he bases it upon a set of hypothetical universal biological characteristics of vertebrates, particularly primates. He says that his argument is true because it applies universally in the vertebrate phylum and must therefore apply to man as well. "Man sooner or later will obey his weapons instinct." (*African Genesis,* p. 326) Lorenz' argument is not based on such absolutism. He does not lose sight of the fact, as does Ardrey, that natural selection favors different responses under different environmental conditions. Lorenz also argues for a widespread aggressive instinct, but for him the proof that it exists in man depends upon evidence from human behavior. On the other hand, as we shall soon see, Lorenz is not unwilling to make facile analogies between what he *thinks geese feel* and what he *thinks men feel* when either species displays this or that overt behavioral pattern.

It is not until the last chapter of *African Genesis* that Ardrey has second thoughts. He tells us that "the human mind stands free, in the sense that it is the servant of no given instinct. In the debate continually raging within us, one instinct may and will act to inhibit another." (p. 354) But "Conscience as a guiding force in the human drama is one of such small reliability that it assumes very nearly the role of villain . . . and if mankind survives the contemporary predicament, it will be in spite of, not because of, the parochial powers of our animal conscience." (p. 355)

Thus behavioral differences between humans are not due to learning, and ethics has little relationship to culture. Ardrey's determinism rests entirely on biological principles, or rather on those few which he favors, and man's social situation contributes little of importance to the stream of history. Even the role of environment in the unfolding of that part of man's existence which is totally biological is ignored.

*On Aggression* by Konrad Lorenz is a somewhat more modest book than Ardrey's. Lorenz does not pretend to have all the answers to the puzzle of human existence. It is also much more scientific. Thus, while Lorenz writes in more moderate tones than Ardrey, in a sense his work is all the more dramatic for that very reason. For Lorenz, who has spent much of his life studying the behavior of birds, aggression is a key to the understanding of social structure in animals. Its function is useful in maintaining social equilibrium and it is only in man, because of culture (rightly seen as a nonhereditary form of adaptation), that aggression provides the basis for self-destruction. Thus, for Lorenz, the dialectic is one of conflict between man's basic biological drives, particularly the aggressive drive, with his exaggerated culture means of displaying it, and human ethical systems which are, if properly developed, capable of containing it.

Lorenz sees the main function of aggression as the geographical spacing of animals of the same species so that their environmental niche may be best exploited. To this main function he adds the possibility of sexual selection in which mates are chosen on the basis of some characteristic, in this case the possession of breeding territory, so that the stronger of two rivals may take possession of it. Aggression can also directly select the strongest individuals through fights, and it has a social function; the protection of young.

Lorenz sees aggression in all animals, including man, as a spontaneous instinct which must find gratification:

"If stimuli to release it fail to appear for an appreciable period, the organism as a whole is thrown into a state of general unrest and begins to search actively for the missing stimulus." (Lorenz, *On Aggression,* p. 50)

The evidence for this theory depends with one exception upon material from animal behavior only and the exception, as we shall see below, is untenable. Lorenz employs the disarming technique of anthropomorphizing the animals he so obviously loves, and at the same time reduces man to the level of the model which assumes animals to be complete automatons. The result is peculiar. Geese feel love and jealousy. Scapegoat behavior in humans is seen as closely analogous to behavior in certain types of fish! Man is trapped by his instincts and culture becomes an impediment to development. Human beings would have been happier if they had remained in a state of nature when instinct would have served man's needs without the dangerous and distorting effect of tradition.

In spite of what Lorenz says, analogous aggressive responses in certain of the lower animals and in man differ in an important respect. In animals careful observation reveals that specific releasing stimuli always elicit a particular response. In man the situation is quite different. Releasers, far from being automatic, are learned. This can be said absolutely, for such releasers are symbols defined in a personal and/or cultural way. For human beings the same stimuli may be either neutral, aggression stimulating, or have some other symbolic function, depending upon what has been learned by the individual. And what has been learned will depend upon culture plus idiosyncratic experiences. In contrast, it is the very predictability of response to specific stimuli which makes Lorenz' animal data look so convincing.

Lorenz believes that under conditions of deprivation certain responses, including aggression, will occur even without releasers. Can we be sure that no external stimuli have led to a specific observed behavior? In the case of human beings, at the very least, this would be a dangerous conclusion. Indeed there is evidence that an aggressive response in animals, including man, can be elicited only with external stimulation, that is, the presence of some environmentally based releaser. This puts aggression in a different class from such drives as sex and hunger, in which internal chemical changes in the organic system produce searching behavior (but not a sterotypic response). The physiological and chemical changes which one can monitor during an aggressive episode come only after some external stimulus has triggered the response.

In *The Territorial Imperative* Ardrey supports Lorenz' view and suggests that internal automatic stimulation has been demonstrated for the aggressive instinct. He cites experiments in which animals' brains were directly stimulated either electrically or chemically to produce aggression. But this does not prove that self stimulation arises *spontaneously* within the organism. The experiment demonstrates only that such animals are capable of responding aggressively. The source of stimuli is still external, although it skips one step in the usual process of release by acting directly on the brain. Ultimately all behavior whether based on drives or on learning must have some chemical–electrical releaser in brain tissue itself. The absence of such central nervous system response potential would mean that the animal could never behave in the expected manner, for the brain would then be blind to the stimulus. Chemical stimulation of the brain, then, merely proves that the organism is potentially capable of those responses that such stimulation releases.

Lorenz draws an analogy between ritual in animals and ritual in man. He sees ritual as a means of channeling aggression into harmless behavior patterns, through the mechanism of displacement. Aggressive energy finds its outlet in the dramatic play involved in ritual rather than in an actual attack. This gives displacement its own survival value. But displacement in animals usually occurs when an expected response is blocked or prevented in some way through either conflicts, such as fear, or some kind of external restraint. Human ritual is much more variable than this. Lacking direct empirical evidence on the relationship between human rituals and displacement in animals, Lorenz creates a just-so story, or origin myth, of the peace pipe ceremony of the American Indian.

Spotted Wolf and Piebald Eagle meet to make peace. One of them, embarrassed and unable to find appropriate words in the tense situation, takes his pipe and begins to smoke. At some future meeting one of the chiefs lights his pipe immediately. Gradually it becomes traditional that a pipe-smoking Indian is more ready to negotiate than a nonsmoking one. It may have taken centuries for the symbol of pipe smoking to mean peace. But Lorenz is quite certain that in the course of

time the original gesture developed into a ritual which pro-
hibited aggression after pipe smoking.

Even if this story were true the behavior described is far
removed from the fixed action patterns of animals, the discovery of which constitutes one of Lorenz' major contributions to
biological studies.

I think Lorenz is correct when he sees ritual as a form of
social communication. But there is no evidence that as such
ritual operates universally or even commonly to reduce aggression. It would appear more likely that ritual has manifold
functions, the most important of which may be instruction in
the symbolic system of the group and the formation of ingroup bonds. As far as aggression is concerned, ritual is just
as likely to aggravate it as it is to reduce it. There is a great
deal of evidence that ritual performances often are used before attacks to increase the fervor of those involved. Just what
is the purpose of a war dance, for example, if not to prepare
participants for war?

Lorenz draws another analogy, this time between ritualized
fighting in vertebrates and the development of morality in
man. He thus attempts to link thinking which demands a
complex ability to symbol particular to man with types of
behavior seen in lower animals. For Lorenz animals display
morality because they do not kill each other in mock fights.
The development of this response in lower animals prepares
the genetic path for later developments in human behavior.

In a later chapter entitled "Rats," Lorenz describes one of
man's most ubiquitous pests in terms which suggest a morality play. The allegory is plain and the message equally clear.
Rats are one of the few species (man is another) in which
collective aggression by one community against another oc-

curs. But the experimental evidence cited is marred because
it is based upon artificial laboratory conditions. This is a serious problem, since among the many insights provided by
Lorenz and other ethologists is the lesson that laboratory experiments often distort behavior. The results are often artifacts of experimental conditions.

Lorenz places great stress upon the bond which develops
among social animals in the same group and its relationship
to aggression between different groups. Here he indulges in a
kind of dialectic in which a specific behavior has its own opposite out of which further patterns are developed.

He then makes the expected jump to man: "Poets and psy-
choanalysts alike have long known how close love and hate
are and we know that in human beings, also, the object of
love is nearly always in an ambivalent way the object of aggression too. The triumph ceremony of geese—and this cannot be stressed too often—is at most an extremely simplified
model of human friendship, but it shows significantly how
such ambivalence can arise." (*On Aggression,* p. 203)

Lorenz goes on to suggest that a personal bond, friendship,
is found only in animals with highly developed aggression.
The firmness of the bond is said to increase with the aggressive level of the animal species. Finally, love arose from intraspecific aggression through ritualization of a redirected attack or threat. These rites are tied to the existence of a
partner. The partner itself is an animal with home valency (it
has the same emotional value as home). Intraspecific aggression can exist without love, but there can be no love without
aggression.

Most psychologists would cavil at this. It is almost impossible to define love or friendship in any operationally meaningful way in lower animals. Even in man the subjectivity of

these concepts creates problems. What is the difference, for example, between affection and love, and what are the differences between love for spouse or mistress, love between parents and children, between siblings, between friends, and between a man or woman and mankind? Such concepts, cloaked as they are in the mystery of metaphor, tell us much about the poetic nature of man but they are useless in an analysis of similarities and differences between human behavior and the behavior of lower animals.

Lorenz throws caution to the wind, however, and tells us that "hate," as opposed to ordinary aggression, is directed toward one individual. Since this is also the case in love, hate equals love. The logic of this escapes me entirely. Equivalences cannot be drawn this way.

The ultimate in argument by metaphor and the anthropomorphization of our animal cousins occurs when Lorenz equates man and greylag geese. He suggests that in geese and man such complex forms of behavior as falling in love, striving for power, jealously, and grieving are the same down to the most absurd details.

These "instincts" are never shown to be automatic in man. The instinct concept in fact runs entirely contrary to a series of experiments conducted by Harry Harlow on the rhesus monkey. Harlow found that the socialization process is crucial to "normal" nurturance behavior in a group. In the initial phase of his experiment Harlow concentrated on security and comforting stimuli in comparison with food provision in mother–infant relationships. Infant monkeys were separated from their mothers and placed in cages equipped with two types of surrogate mothers. One of these, a wire mother, was made of rough wire surmounted with a schematized wooden face. The other surrogate mother was soft and cuddly, covered with terry cloth, and had a more monkeylike face. Eight newborn monkeys were placed in individual cages. Each had equal access to a cloth and a wire mother. Four of the infants received milk from one mother and four from the other. The milk was furnished by a nursing bottle, its nipple protruding from the mother's "breast."

The two mothers were physiologically equivalent. All the monkeys drank the same amount of milk and gained weight at the same rate. On the other hand, the two mothers were psychologically distinct. Records showed that all infants spent far more time climbing and clinging to the cloth mothers than to the wire mothers. Those that fed from the wire mother spent no more time on her than required for feeding. This contradicted the idea that affection is learned or derived in association with the reduction of hunger or thirst.

Harlow found that under stress conditions the infant would automatically seek comfort from the cloth mother. The most interesting and surprising results, however, came as an unanticipated consequence of this set of experiments. In a later paper, Harlow described the behavior of those animals which had been deprived of normal nurturant relationships with real mothers.

> As month after month and year after year have passed, these monkeys have appeared to be less and less normal. We have seen them sitting in their cages strangely mute, staring fixedly into space, relatively indifferent to people and other monkeys. Some clutch their heads in both hands and rock back and forth—the autistic behavior pattern that we have seen in babies raised on wire surrogates. Others, when approached or even left alone, go into violent frenzies of rage, grasping and tearing at their legs with such fury that they sometimes require medical care.
>
> Eventually we realized that we had a laboratory full of neu-

rotic monkeys. . . ." (Harlow, "Heterosexual Affectional System in Monkeys," p. 6)

> We deliberately initiated a breeding program which was frighteningly unsuccessful. When the older, wire-cage raised monkeys were paired with the females at the peak of estrus, the introduction led only to fighting, so violent and vicious that separation was essential to survival. In no case was there any indication of normal sex behavior. Frequently the females were the aggressors; even the normal praying mantis waits until the sex act is completed. (*Ibid.*, p. 7)

In an attempt to overcome the effects of abnormal socialization Harlow then began a reeducation program for both female and male monkeys. Neurotic males were exposed to mature and calm normal females; female monkeys were exposed to sexually adequate but gentle males.

> When the laboratory-bred females were smaller than the sophisticated males, the girls would back away and sit down facing the males, looking appealingly at these would be consorts. Their hearts were in the right place, but nothing else was. When the females were larger than the males, . . . they would attack and maul the ill-fated male.
>
> The training program for the males was equally unsatisfactory. They approached the females with blind enthusiasm. Frequently the males would grasp the females by the side of the body and thrust laterally, leaving them working at cross purposes with reality. Even the most persistent attempts by these females to set the boys straight came to naught. (*Ibid.*, p. 7)

It is clear that abnormal socialization leads to a range of abnormal behaviors affecting the proper functioning of the sex drive and the development of what Harlow refers to as the heterosexual affectional system. It is also apparent from this material that aggressive behavior is at least in part a product of the socialization process. Comparing these two aspects of behavior we see that the sex drive persists but its expression is hopelessly distorted while the expression or nonexpression of aggression is an outcome of social variables.

Response thresholds appear to vary with the socialization experience as well as the type of stimulus which will induce an animal to respond aggressively. There is some genetic control over this process, but environmental modification is so pronounced that to speak of an aggressive instinct merely masks the difficulty inherent in the analytic task. Once aroused (through certain stimuli), aggression is a likely but not exclusive response of an organism. If aggressive behavior is related genetically to threshold levels, we can see why environment plays so important a role in its expression. Most thresholds can be modified through experience. Also animals can be trained to respond to particular sign stimuli and to ignore others.

Now let it be perfectly clear that I am speaking about aggression in primates and man. There may be a closer tie between particular natural stimuli and aggressive response in other families of the animal kingdom, tied to both territoriality and sexual union. But one of the major tendencies of evolution has been the development of behavioral flexibility which allows organisms to change patterns of behavior in response to local conditions. A large repertoire of fixed action patterns guarantees an animal adaptive responses under certain specific environmental conditions, but such rigidity may be maladaptive under variable conditions. Learning capacities allow for rapid environmental accommodations. Organisms without culture cannot pass specific learning episodes on to their progeny, but selection can favor an increased genetic capacity for such learning as well as increased flexibility of response.

Learning through experience is not the only way in which behavior can be modified. Harlow's experiments show that various types of early experience may affect an animal's behavior in relation to another set of experiences later in life. Carlton Gajdusek (in a personal communication) has shown me an amazing set of readouts on behavior observed in mice of the same genetic strain raised under varying sets of laboratory conditions. These conditions included removal from the mother at different stages of maturation and development in isolation from siblings for different periods and at different times in the maturation process. In every case, slight variations in early socialization had their affect on a range of later behaviors, including aggressive responses. The unfolding of behavior is a complex process of development. Certain genetic backgrounds may set probability levels for certain degrees and types of responses under controlled environmental conditions. In some cases these probability levels may be 100 percent, but they can be much lower. When environmental conditions are varied the expression of the gene may also vary to a considerable extent. Observation of behavior under natural conditions is not adequate for the analysis of such environment–genetic interactions. What appear to be fixed patterns in nature may occur only in relation to a normal unfolding of events.

Lorenz is, of course, familiar with the interaction between genetics and learning. Yet when he discusses aggression in man and other animals he reverts to a static model of genetic control. Culture can, he admits, change the direction and expression of the aggressive drive, but the drive must be expressed regardless of conditions.

In contrast psychoanalytic theory (even for those who accept an aggressive instinct) is based on the idea that early experience has a profound effect upon later performance and

the process of psychoanalysis involves a resocialization of individuals through the careful attention of an understanding
and supporting parental substitute. Human beings equipped
with the symbolic process can do something which Harlow's
monkeys are incapable of. They can repeat their childhood
and symbolically reformulate their personalities. Such reformation can lead to a new set of adaptive responses. Normal
humans like normal monkeys are produced through the unfolding of a social process in which mutually rewarding nurturant experience is the rule.

Lorenz' counter argument to this point is that progressive—permissive education does not lower aggressive levels
in children. This fails to take account of the primary home
experience. In addition, many progressive schools face the
problem of competition for the affection of the parental surrogate, the teacher. This can be intense among rather large
numbers of children of the same age and similar needs in
the same classroom. Furthermore, Lorenz does not investigate the possibility that in schools like Summerhill children
who experience a permissive atmosphere also experience the
kind of noncompetitive socialization which appears in fact to
produce well adjusted, relatively nonaggressive adults. Finally we are provided with no empirical evidence as to the
similarities or differences between children educated in progressive schools and children who were the products of the
"normal" educational process.

As I pointed out in chapter 1, Lorenz is out to attack social
science. The best he can do is to destroy a straw man. He
suggests that social scientists have erected three obstacles to
self knowledge: 1) by their refusal to admit that man is an
animal, 2) by their refusal to admit that man is part of the
evolutionary process, and 3) by their refusal to accept the

fact that natural law governs human behavior. While it is partially true that some sociologists and a few psychologists have been guilty of ignoring the first two points, all social scientists see their task as the search for laws of behavior. If sociologists have ignored biology, it is only because they have chosen to concentrate on social phenomena. This is clearly not a successful method of solving all problems, but it can be applied to many within the traditional framework of sociological research. When we turn to anthropology, particularly American anthropology, Lorenz' accusations become patently false. Cultural anthropology has, for good empirical reasons, rejected the idea that the significant behavioral differences among different social groups can be explained on the basis of biological laws. Instead they have used biology to sort out underlying similarities—those principles which provide the biological basis for human behavior. At the present time there is a reawakening of interest in the contribution which biological factors make to differences in behavior, as well, but the approach is more complicated and sophisticated than the one which Lorenz himself proposes. Man is seen as an animal, but with a unique set of species specific traits based on culture which can only be explained in the context of general biological and evolutionary theory.

What are the biological principles which Lorenz wishes to substitute for culture? They are nothing more than arguments by analogy. Thus we find that the origin of a higher form of life from a simpler ancestor means an increase in values. This is "a reality as undeniable as our own existence." A pretty turn of phrase but no scientific statement. Morality is by its very nature dependent upon a complex process of symbolization, and so when Lorenz says "for a man who finds it equally

easy to chop up a live dog and a live lettuce I would recom-
mend suicide at his earliest convenience," I would respond
"true enough," but add that any chimpanzee who finds it
equally easy to chop up a live dog and a live lettuce is in
fact a normal chimpanzee. The restraints against killing
among nonhumans usually, if not always, extend only to
members of one's own species. Any chimp who displayed
the morality of men would have either to be a man or have
been trained by men. In the latter case the inhibitions would
not be based on morality but would have been induced by
careful training. Lorenz is certainly aware that restraints
upon killing which exist among most human groups are subject to modification through learning. The Nazis discovered
that people could be conditioned to accept the idea that
some people were different enough from them (if not lettuce,
at any rate subhuman) so that inhibitions to mass murder
could be removed. Morality did not evolve through phylogeny but out of culture, a system endowed with the *capacity* for the development of some kind of morality.

It is only towards the end of *On Aggression* that Lorenz
turns completely to man. He wants to know why reasonable
beings behave so unreasonably. This contrasts with the question which anthropologists ask: what are the reasons behind
human action? When the question is put in Lorenz' terms it
precludes the possibility that what appear to be unrational
behaviors are not only subject to natural law, but represent
adaptive forms of behavior in relation to particular sets of environmental circumstances. Lorenz never asks if destructive
or aggressive behavior might be due not to biopsychological
factors on the level of the individual organism but rather to
socio-economic factors external to the individual. It is important for his argument that certain aspects of behavior remain
irrational since for him they are caused by the contradictions

inherent in the conflict between knowledge and instinct. For Lorenz the roots of evil lie in original sin and not in social conditions. Men are like rats, pacifistic in their own groups, but hostile to all other groups. This is the normal state of being human, the state of being that must be overcome if we are to survive as a species.

Lorenz jumps from the truth that cultural evolution outstrips biological evolution (because it is a more efficient process) to the assumption that for this reason social inhibitions based on biological factors cannot keep pace with technological change. He argues that while many dangerous animals have instinctive inhibitions against killing their own species, man lacks such inhibitions because, as an animal, he is incapable of sudden killing, physiologically and morphologically. The development of weapons gives man the "accidental capability" of killing his fellow man. I can only agree that man has no instinctive inhibition against killing (and also no other instincts which drive him to kill), but neither this nor aggression can account for war.

Humans have not yet killed themselves off, according to Lorenz, because responsibility and morality are also achievements of the human facility, "asking questions." From this argument comes the assumption that the invention of artificial weapons has "brought about a most undesirable predominance of intraspecific selection within mankind." The strongest have survived, the most aggressive have survived, the warlike instinct has survived at the expense of more morally or pacifistically inclined individuals. As we shall see in a later chapter this theory ignores all the evidence for counter selection in the evolution of man. It also ignores the fact that under most conditions a good soldier is disciplined and passive, ready to take orders, rather than aggressive.

The culmination of *On Aggression* hinges upon a single

study among Indians of the Ute tribe. This material is used to prove that natural selection has operated to favor the development of an extreme aggressive drive and that the blockage of aggression produces a situation in which Indians suffer more frequently from neurosis than any other human group. The cause of this neurosis is said to be undischarged aggression.

Where are the controls? How do we know that this tribe suffers more frequently than any other from neurosis? With how many groups has Lorenz compared them? Anthropologists familiar with the Ute Indians find no similarity between what they know of the Utes and the unpublished study reported by Lorenz.

> Plains and prairie Indian ethno-history does not reveal that those people led a wild life consisting almost entirely of wars and raids. They had war and they did raid, but their history was not of such war and raiding as to make them unique among social groups. The Ute Indians were early horsemen and hunted buffalo on the High Plains. While there, they were prepared to fight or run, and they always returned to the Rocky Mountains and maintained their homes there. In early historic times, they were often referred to as the "Swiss" Indians.
>
> The implication that these Ute were a violent people, addicted to war, is not borne out by historic facts. With the early Spanish settlers the Utes were primarily friendly traders; later, they had amicable relations with Americans. In 1776, the Utes guided Escalante through their territory; in 1806, they guided Pike. They were collaborators with the American trappers following the Louisiana Purchase and the explorations of Lewis and Clark. During the Civil War, they served as paid scouts and allies of the U.S. Army in wars against plains tribes, and the Navaho, yet immediately after these skirmishes, they made visits to the same tribes and welcomed return visits. The Utes collaborated with the U.S. government

in nearly every way and became aggressive only under extreme provocation, such as when betrayed by agent Meeker and threatened by an unwarranted armed invasion of their reservation in 1879.

The Utes not only were not addicted to unusual "violence toward people not of their own tribe," but they did not have a rule that "anyone killing a member of the tribe was compelled by strict traditions to commit suicide." I have known personally four Utes who killed fellow Utes; none committed suicide. One, living on the Southern Ute Reservation in 1964, was convicted of murdering his uncle who was a policeman. He had served time in a Federal prison and was on parole. A similar case was a Ute who had killed his wife. Suicides and attempted suicides among the Ute have not been murderers of fellow tribesmen. (Omar C. Stewart, "Lorenz/Margolin on the Ute," pp. 105–6).

Margolin's statements of fact which are subject to testing concerning the Ute Indians are simply not correct. Others are questionable. Has Margolin the statistics to substantiate the claim that "Ute Indians suffer more frequently from neurosis than any other human group"? As a group, the Ute Indians seem to differ slightly from other people in a number of ways. These differences are not great, or sensational, or sweeping. They are, however, based on painstakingly collected facts, established by psychologists and sociologists, as well as anthropologists, using carefully prepared interview guides, selected samples, and statistical analysis. These are contained in the reports of the Tri-ethnic project published or in press under the names of Richard Jessor, Robert Hansen, and Theodore Graves.

Finally the peyote religion of the Ute is a significant refutation of the Lorenz-Margolin thesis. The Ute appear to have been receptive to peyote as early as 1900, according to Mooney, who reported their participation in the peyote ritual with the Jicarilla Apache. Their interest grew by means of visits to Taos and Oklahoma until the cult was firmly established, especially on the Ute Mountain Ute Reservation in southwestern

Colorado, where it flourished from 1916 on. The peyote religion is a syncretistic cult, incorporating ancient Indian and
modern Christian elements. The Christian theology of love,
charity, and forgiveness has long been added to the ancient
Indian ritual and aboriginal desire to acquire personal power
through individual visions. Peyotism has taught a program of
accommodation for over 50 years and the peyote religion has
succeeded in giving Indians pride in their native culture while
adjusting to the dominant civilization of the whites. (*Ibid.*, pp.
107–8)

To be consistent with Margolin's scheme, one must assume
that only those who were aggressive would be permitted to
mate. To accomplish this, fulfillment of a criterion of aggressivity through participation in warfare or other aggressive behavior would have to have been a prerequisite to marriage.

These assumptions are not supportable. Insofar as inbreed-
ing is concerned, we find that Ute marital patterns are not
solely Ute or Ute prairie-tribe marriages. As a matter of fact,
the Ute engaged in some warfare, basically raids, which were
carried out primarily for the purpose of women stealing.
These raids were made on non-Prairie Pueblos. The Pueblos
have long been described as non-aggressive. Ruth Benedict
contrasts their peaceable nature with that of other Indian
groups, pointing out their lack of tolerance of violence. They
are believers in moderation and will have nothing to do with
disruptive individual experience.

Rockwell states that in addition to outmarriages with the
Pueblo tribes, the Ute also married the non-Prairie Bannock
and Snake Indians living to the West. This would further invalidate the conclusion of Lorenz and Margolin, since it was
stated that only prairie tribes "were subject to the selection
pressures described." Since the Bannock and Snake or Pueblo
Indians do not qualify for the "selection pressures", we must
assume that they are not aggressive peoples and are, therefore, introducing genetically different material into the Ute
gene pool. (John Beatty, "Taking Issue with Lorenz on the
Ute," pp. 112–13)

This is a crucial argument, since Lorenz has attempted to provide a behavioral–genetic basis for an understanding of Ute social behavior. If the marriage patterns do not conform to the process which Lorenz and Margolin describe, the entire hypothesis is invalid.

The inability of Lorenz to connect his hypothesis rigorously to sound genetic data is no more obvious than in his contention that intraspecific selection is still operating in an undesirable direction. He says that there is a high positive selection premium for instinctive traits such as the amassing of property, self-assertion, etc., and that there is an almost equally high negative premium on simple goodness. He warns that competition in business threatens to fix in us hypertrophies of these traits as horrible as the intraspecific aggression evolved by competition between warfaring tribes of stone age man. He sees some hope in the fact that the accumulation of riches and power usually correlates with small families. If this were not so "the future of mankind would look even darker than it does." That's the whole point! Eugenists have been saying for years that the most undesirable traits occur in those individuals who reproduce in the greatest numbers, but careful examination of birth statistics show that this is rarely if ever the case. If such traits are not present among the fecund they cannot increase in the population at the expense of other traits. Lorenz deflects criticism by telling us that morality does not derive from rationality—as if anyone said that it did. Experiments such as those carried out by Harlow suggest that morality is a product of socialization. Certainly a morality which considers the worth and life of others grows out of the ability of individuals to feel empathy and act altruistically. Analogous behavior may operate in lower species to preserve the lives and therefore the genes of close relatives, but it is only among humans that an individual will sacrifice himself for the good of a nonrelative. Such a phenomenon cannot have a positive selective value, since an individual with "an altruistic gene" would actually be more likely than others to be sorted out during selection. Those who sacrifice themselves sacrifice their genes as well. Selection demands that an individual survive long enough to pass his genes on to the next generation and in greater numbers than others not sharing a particular trait. Empathy and morality can only have a value for survival after man *qua* man has emerged and the human type of sociocultural system has been established. The capacity for empathy and morality exists in man as a byproduct of both his genetic structure and his social existence. Any particular expression of morality will be defined by culture.

Lorenz leaves us with questions which can be answered, as he covertly admits, by anthropologists rather than by specialists in animal behavior. It is quite certain, he says, that natural selection rather than insight gave rise to traditional norms and rights. "Historians will have to face the fact that natural selection determines the evolution of cultures in the same manner as it did that of species." (*On Aggression*, p. 251)

On this point I agree, but, as I hope to show, that process is far more complicated than either Ardrey or Lorenz would have us believe. Lorenz correctly sees an interaction between the need for adaptive change and the rigidity of norms in society, but he goes astray when he says that the means by which a compromise can be struck between these two opposing forces is prescribed by biological laws "of the widest range of application." It is precisely here that more research needs to be done and it is precisely here that Lorenz fails us. The accurate cataloging of biological needs provides only the barest beginning in a search for understanding. Far from being prescribed by biological laws in the sense that Lorenz intends, man is free to exploit his vast range of biological capacities, for as surely as man is born with a *capacity* for aggression, he is also born with a capacity for empathy and sympathy, a capacity for nonviolence, and a capacity for exploratory behavior expressed in curiosity and its behavioral consequences. Man is also born with the capacity for abstract thinking: to use language and to create and to experiment. Whether or not and how these various capacities are to be expressed is dependent upon the individual's social experiences in the family and in wider social groups. The bonds placed on man are placed by other men and by the forces of culture which as a system is responsive to the natural and the social environment. Culture is not free of biology. On the contrary, human behavioral systems must adapt the way species adapt to environments or be weeded out in the process of natural selection. It is the laws of natural selection governing the process of cultural evolution which must be investigated along with the evolution of man's capacities and their roots in the biological past.

In spite of his frequent elegance and apparent humanism, Lorenz' vision reflects bewilderment over the rapidity of modern social change. Thus he views adolescent rebellion as the result of instinctive need to be the member of a closely knit group. In addition, "fighting for common ideals may grow so strong that it becomes inessential what these ideals are and whether they possess any intrinsic value." (*On Aggression*, p. 258)

And this process takes effect only once in an individual's life. Once the allegiance to a certain cause is fixed, it cannot be replaced by a new one of equal strength.

Ideology is supported by another biological characteristic (Lorenz says "autonomous instinct") of man: "militant enthusiasm." This is said to develop out of the communal defense response. Militant enthusiasm frequently manifests itself in adolescents who are on the threshold of adulthood and responsibility. They are of the group and apart from it. They question the values of their parents and society at large and they may form into gangs if social pressures imposed upon them by the adult world frustrate and antagonize them. Militant enthusiasm has its own appetitive behavior and its own releasing mechanisms; its expression engenders feelings of intense satisfaction.

Such a conception begs several questions. What are the appetitive behaviors associated with militant enthusiasm and what are the specific releasing mechanisms? It turns out that the stimulus situation is the automatic division into opposing camps which functions "to arouse militant enthusiasm in a satisfying manner." It would follow that political parties are organized unconsciously by human beings to provide themselves with an outlet for an instinct which must be satisfied. Is this not turning things a bit inside out?

Lorenz maintains an optimistic point of view, but his solutions to the problem of human aggression are disappointing. They represent all the old clichés about increased peaceful competition and the appreciation of specific capabilities in groups other than one's own. This approach is nowhere better expressed than in his suggestion that "the universal appreciation of Negro music is perhaps an important step towards the solution of the burning racial problem in America." (*On Aggression*, p. 278) This is followed by the statement that humor exerts a moral influence on social behavior. I'm sure it does, but in what direction? Joking certainly can be used to relieve tensions and create amity between hostile individuals and groups, but the race joke, for example, which derides the characteristics of another human being, certainly serves as the handmaiden of aggression.

Lorenz fails to see that enmity has its roots deep in the social process, that it is frequently the result of economic exploitation, and that the stereotypes which foster intergroup differences refer back to the situation in which men exploit other men, often without hatred or aggressive feelings, but rather with little awareness *or feeling* for the exploited.

# IS TERRITORIALITY
# IMPERATIVE?

*The Territorial Imperative* constitutes a further extension of the Lorenz-Ardrey aggression-territory hypothesis and a review of the biological studies on territorial behavior in infrahuman species. Territory is defined as "an area of space, whether of water or earth or air, which an animal or group of animals defends as an exclusive" (p. 3). Less satisfactory is the statement: "The word is also used to describe the inward compulsion in animate beings to possess and defend such a space." A territorial species is defined as "one in which all males and sometimes females too bear an inherent drive to gain and defend an exclusive property" (p. 3). Considering what has already been said about aggression, we must ask what is meant by inward compulsion. Does territorial behavior appear automatically as the result of chemical changes within the organism which produce a "need for release"? Is it an automatic response which occurs only in the presence of some specific external releaser? Or is it a variable pattern of behavior which results from the interaction of genetic coding and experience? And above all, is what can be defined as territorial behavior in a wide range of species necessarily the same response or does a single definition beg the question and obscure differences? Ardrey's argument runs like this. For at least some animals territorial behavior appears to be innate. Since territorial behavior appears in many species, it must be adaptive and therefore an essential element in evolution. Territoriality exists for so many species that it must also exist for man, since he is also a species. Finally, any behavior in human groups which is in any way connected with property or territory is evidence for the drive in man. Evidence against a universal drive for territory in human history is taken as either incorrect or a momentary aberration of man's basic biological structure which is detrimental to human survival. Thus, while Lorenz attempts to account for evil on the basis of a not incurable imcompatibility between biology and culture Ardrey sees the drive alone as essential, not only as an explanation of human existence, but as the major *raison d'être* of man. Schools of behavioral analysis which condemn either the instinct concept or man's lust for territory, whenever it occurs, are playing a wicked game, says Ardrey, because they inhibit that which cannot be inhibited and lead man along a biologically dangerous political path.

The territorial drive is exclusive of, and takes precedence over, the sex drive. It is, in fact, used by Ardrey as the primal explanatory principle in animal behavior. Even aggression is secondary to territoriality and operates in its service.

Territoriality has a multitude of survival values. It offers security from predators, it insures adequate food supply, and it operates in sexual selection, for it is only the male who possesses territory who can mate. It also acts as a force in the development of group cohesion in social species and provides a source of excitement and stimulation (particularly in certain bird species) through the dramatic expression of border quarrels.

Ardrey must account for the fact that territorial behavior takes different forms. Territoriality is defined as an instinct with an open program. The instinct must be satisfied but the behavioral path to satisfaction is determined by learning and, in the case of man, by culture. In practice, however, Ardrey allows fewer degrees of freedom for the expression of this "instinct" than the data demands. He ignores the fact that the most primitive societies, those which depend on hunting and gathering, are the least territorial of all human groups. Private property is the child of culture and develops into a major preoccupation only with the evolution of complex society. Allegiance to territory rather than to one's kin is a relatively recent development in human history, accompanying the invention of the state. Rules for opting in or out of established territories (laws of immigration and emigration, adoption, rules for naturalization, etc.) and systems of signs and markers (symbols of nationhood and in many cases rules against treason) were established to reinforce culturally defined territoriality. If territoriality were "natural" for man it would also be automatic, yet when territoriality becomes imperative for particular human groups, national conscience is systematically developed through enculturation to insure the continuity of the system. The amount of unconscious as well as conscious effort that goes into this process, from the learning of the pledge of allegiance and the rules of behavior concerning the flag (nowhere else so strict as in the United States) to the passing of military conscription laws to insure the defense of national interests, militates against the automatic and instinctive nature of territoriality.

Ardrey's lack of understanding of the heredity–environment interaction process is so profound that even his data on nonhuman species amounts to a distortion of biological reality. He is not only wrong about man but, in most cases, is wrong or, better, overly simplistic about the behavior of lower animals. Thus I differ from those critics who see *The Territorial Imperative* as inapplicable to man but as an excellent review of territoriality in animals.

As an instinct territoriality obeys several laws which allow us to predict history. Ardrey, as we shall see below, has an amazing capacity to predict events *ex post facto*. Let us look at these "laws" to see if they fit the facts and if they are capable of generating useful predictions. My comments are in parentheses.

1. Animals do not compete for females but only for territory. (Remember the wife raids of the Ute? Raiding for females is *not* an isolated esoteric phenomenon in man. In fact, the fierce Yanamomö recently described by Napoleon Chagnon fight over women.)

2. The holder of a particular territory is generally victorious over the challenger. (Compare this to the outcome of human wars.)

3. The holder of a particular territory holds a psychological advantage. This reduces the probability that fighting will occur. (This appears to be true of some infrahuman species and demonstrates how territoriality and aggressive displays tend to reduce overt conflict.)

4. When an individual is removed from or leaves his terri-

tory there is no antagonism displayed between individuals. (This applies to those animals which are seasonally territorial and has no relationship to human behavior. Some human groups construct *cultural* rules of safe conduct for individuals in times of war, but these serve socio-economic or political ends, do not apply universally, and hence cannot be instinctual.)

5. Sexual desire in males and females occurs only in connection with territorial possession. (This has no relationship to human behavior.)

6. A group of territorial animals holds allegiance to its specific territory. (This is true by definition and is circular.)

7. Most males who fail to obtain territory of their own join bachelor herds, but some succeed in establishing their own territory. These animals tend to be relatively unsuccessful in attracting females. (This has no relationship to human behavior.)

Ardrey displays a clear tendency to confuse what are often complex behavioral patterns among animals, involving manipulation of the environment, with patterns of culture in man. According to Ardrey, the Bower bird and man are physically drab species; therefore they must "invent" and construct that which some species come equipped with naturally. This unfruitful comparison has no bearing upon the evolution of human behavior and it falsely suggests that the Bower bird has culture. The tendency to anthropomorphize animals is frequently encountered among laymen but it is rarely used as an argument by biologists (Lorenz is an exception). The confusion inherent in such metaphorization leads away from a true understanding of what animals and man *do* have in common. This is a problem which I myself have noted. I remember how difficult it was several years ago to convince some of my rather sophisticated but also sentimental Vassar students that birds do not really talk, even though some could be trained to use words. There is an essential difference between innate precoded patterns of behavior, culture, and a learned response to a set of cues which in talking birds are invented by man and not by birds. Man is born with the physical equipment to produce elaborate forms of behavior, but these forms can develop only in the context of a particular tradition and the capacity itself can be thwarted, as we have already seen, through faulty socialization.

Like Lorenz, Ardrey sees a continuity between the evolution of morality in lower animals and its expression in man. Also like Lorenz, he tends to substitute metaphor for empirical evidence. He tells us that "evolution is capable of fostering inborn traits" and that evolution restrains the individual for the ultimate benefit of the species.

Evolution, however, takes place on the level of the individual, for it is in the individual organism that the variation necessary for evolutionary change occurs. Since individual organisms are subject to the vicissitudes of historical accident, the process of adaptation is a statistical one. Biologists can only predict the mathematical chances that a certain gene will be maintained in successive generations, grow, or diminish in frequency, under given conditions. They cannot predict that each organism endowed with a "superior" gene will outreproduce individuals with "inferior" genetic material. Organisms inhabiting an ecological niche do affect each other's life chances, and statistical expectations refer to populations rather than individuals. Thus, biologists refer to the population as the unit of evolution, but this does not mean that evolution *restrains* the individual for the good of the species.

Ardrey is aware that modern Darwinian theory is concerned more with selective fertility (differential reproduction)
than with selective mortality. In fact, he uses this concept to
account for the pair bond between animals of the opposite
sex which he says evolved as a specific mechanism to protect
offspring. Pair bonding is tied to territoriality through the
suggestion that such bonds originate between males and females on a territory which the mating pair holds in common.
The territorial bond provides insurance that the offspring will
be cared for. However, in many species which display territoriality on a seasonal basis, space is held only until such time
as the female is impregnated. The mates then part until the
advent of another mating season. The young remain attached
to their mothers through the period of their immaturity. Furthermore, pair bonds exist in many nonterritorial species and
in some of these persist throughout the year. Finally, there
are territorial species, like the baboon, in which pair bonds
do not form and among which the role of the mother is nurturant, while the role of the male is protective *but* towards all
immature members of the troop.

Human marriage is linked by Ardrey to the desire for a
place of one's own (a territory). He ignores the fact that in
many regions of the world, in many different cultures, a place
of one's own is far from the mind of either member of the
mating pair. In fact, the American ideal, neolocal marriage
(in which the couple sets up an independent household), is
quite rare. More common types of marital residence (the
newlyweds have to live somewhere) are patrilocal, in which
the couple lives with or near the family of the groom's father;
matrilocal, in which they live with or near the territory of the
bride's mother; or avunculocal, in which the married pair
lives with the groom's mother's brother. Such residence rules

are tied to rules of inheritance, social alliances, and sometimes to property, but not in any inherent way. And when they are tied to property it is generally communal rather than individual. The Abron of the Ivory Coast, whom I shall describe later in greater detail, follow a form of residence known as duolocal in which a husband and his wife or wives all live in separate households, those of their respective parents of the same sex. The Abron, however, have no difficulty in raising children and maintaining sexual as well as economic unions. The residence pattern coupled with inheritance rules does, however, have its peculiar effects on the functioning of the social system.

Ardrey bolsters his contention that man is a territorial species by referring to several anonymous biologists who, like him, fail to take culture into account. Of these, one, when asked if he regarded man as a territorial animal, replied, "Yes, certainly. You have only to notice the signboards dotted all over the country announcing that trespassers will be prosecuted." Another said, "Man considers it his inherent right to own property, either as an individual or as a member of a group or both. . . ." Both of these statements illustrate a profound failure to realize that what man considers his inherent right at any particular moment in time and space is itself a product of history. The rules are cultural, not biological. Rules against free access to land were met with disbelief by certain American Indians, and the treaties signed by certain chiefs (often created by the white man for just that purpose) had no meaning to them. The land was there to be used by all, provided that it was respected. In Africa today there are innumerable situations in which peoples of different ethnic backgrounds live together in the same territory, often exploiting the environment in different ways. This *pax indigene* is traditional rather than the result of colonial imposition. Ardrey flies in the face of all these facts to tell us that property relations are the hub of human existence. He tells us that systems of social development that ignored the holding of territory or relied upon systems of involuntary work (slavery, the imposition of the work load on women, etc.) gave way to those based on private property and individual work because they were inefficient. They did not allow for the natural instinct of territoriality to express itself in what Ardrey evidently takes to be its most direct and natural form, that is, capitalism, and small-scale capitalism at that.

Even a slight familiarity with history and social analysis is enough to show that slavery and serfdom were maintained as long as they fitted a specific socio-economic pattern. When this changes, the organization of work changes. Slavery, serfdom, and other productive systems are efficient under specific historical conditions. This is the major message in Marx, and is accepted by most historians in spite of quarrels, political and otherwise, with the rest of Marxian analysis. In anthropology, Julian Steward has demonstrated that patterns related to the organization of work can be seen as specific adaptations to ecological conditions. If, on the other hand, territoriality were instinctive, and if its most perfect expression were in capitalism, we might ask: why did it take so long (two or three million years!) for this basic instinct to find its proper expression in human behavior?

For Ardrey, the incentive which drives man is not only property but affluence: possession of abundance. The anthropologist Marshall Sahlins has shown through a careful analysis of historical and ethnographic material on hunting and gathering bands that such people shun abundant possessions. They prefer to live with a minimum burden of belongings, because inessential property would interfere with their mode of subsistence. Such groups are often familiar with more technologically advanced peoples around them and yet reject a more abundant mode of life. Hunting and gathering need not be a difficult mode of life. Under most conditions the work load is light and food adequate, often superior in protein quality and quantity to that of overworked, starch-eating agriculturists. Many hunters refuse to trade their leisure for affluence. The extinction of hunting society is due to conquest, not choice. Furthermore, although such people enjoy hunting, they do not do it for fun. The land is not overhunted and men prefer to spend their leisure time gambling and telling stories. Recently the Tanzanian government attempted to settle a hunting group, the Hadza, in agricultural villages. The Hadza resisted. They did not want to trade a relatively carefree life to become slaves to the land.

Human beings make decisions about work in the context of their culture and, to some extent, particularly in our own culture, on the basis of individual psychology, drive, and skill. Most of us are prisoners of an ethic in which we are work-driven, and we are also prisoners of an economic system which demands both overproduction and overconsumption. From the strictly biological viewpoint such a system would seem both unsatisfactory and, in the long run, maladaptive. It takes a tremendous psychological toll of individuals and, in addition, has a destructive potential in relation to the environment which is truly frightening. Our system developed under demographic and social conditions which now are beginning to show signs of strain. Even those who are most convinced that capitalism is the only rational economic system have begun to search for means to redirect or limit some of the energy which the system has generated.

Ardrey explains differences in efficiency of production in the Soviet Union and the United States in terms of pride in one's territory. Yet, as C. Wright Mills has pointed out, no matter what we think of the brutalities associated with the Soviet system and no matter how much we condemn its attitude towards human freedom it was, in fact, amazingly efficient given the particular circumstances of precommunist Russia.

In *The Territorial Imperative* Ardrey ignores the industrial side of both the United States and the Soviet Union. Thus he passes over two important, though different, productive systems both of which were successful in generating and using tremendous amounts of energy. He focuses on agriculture because the Soviet Union has continued to have severe agricultural difficulties and because his interpretation of these difficulties fits his theory. It is interesting to note, in this respect, that mainland China has managed to increase agricultural production to the point where growth of output exceeds population increase. Although the experiment is of recent origin, it appears that so far the Chinese have solved a major problem common to third world countries in a way that is contrary to all capitalistic principles.

If one is a strict biological determinist, then differences in human behavioral systems must be explained away or ignored to maintain the biological universal. Ardrey tries to do this but is successful only in creating two major types of human behavioral systems which are set forth as analogous to two different types of animal society. These are the so-called noyau and the nation. Ardrey is never able to explain satisfactorily how a single species guided by instinct manages to split into two basic types of social order, although it is clear that he does not mean to imply that peoples who behave within their groups in one or the other of these ways do so because they are compelled to do so by their genes.

The *noyau* is a society of inward antagonism. The archetype species of the noyau is the *lepilemur* (a primate living only in Madagascar). One lepilemur group defends a territory upon which individual members squabble among themselves and live in total isolation from other such coherent, cohesive, but intra-aggressively active groups. Noyaux are bound together on a specific piece of land in what the author refers to as a dear-enemy relationship. Fighting between individuals provides stimulation and excitement for the members of the group and is therefore adaptive. This is puzzling, for how without some other mechanism can we use the concept of selective fertility to account for the development of such genetic patterning? How would fighting of this type contribute to selective fertility? Ardrey provides no answer. Instead, the need for excitement discovered in lepilemur is immediately translated into human terms and is used to explain why country lads leave their rural homes and seek pleasure in the city. This explanation is then monstrously applied to the dynamics of modern African society. "It is the Kikuyu in Kenya's empty yellow hills or the Zulu in Natal's green slumberland leaving the kralls predictably behind, willingly, joyfully to enlist himself in Nairobi's quarreling mass of unemployed or Johannesburg's crime-ridden, pass-carrying black utopia." (*Territorial Imperative*, p. 173) This is not only vulgar, it is dangerous. For it is historical fact that for every African who goes to the city to seek the "pleasure of the fast life" there are hundreds who are driven there by the simple economic need to pay taxes which were imposed with the express purpose of dragging them into the white industrial complex which functions at the expense of black labor. The hut tax was a clever invention of the white colonialist and its imposition led to a revolution in black social structure. If, on the contrary, the drive for excitement were somehow a biological reality, individuals would have flocked freely to the cities. This kind of simplistic argument is continued and magnified in Ardrey's latest work, *The Social Contract*.

Ardrey presents us with a world vision suspiciously akin to those emotionally tied to nineteenth-century expansionism. It is, to say the least, a dangerous vision, since it presents an anachronistic utopian view of the white man at a time when the world must come to grips with the realities of social and economic history.

Italy is a noyau, for it remains a "patchwork of jealousies, feuds, ambitions, rivalries, and headless horsemen." This type of society however, has a biological advantage and therefore can survive. The noyau is flexible; there is no one authority, no one leader, and it is therefore difficult to put out of operation. Yet we know that in Africa those societies with strong internal coherence and centralized political authority had little difficulty in subjecting kinship-based, societies with no central leadership to their rule. In terms of military organization such societies have little chance in the face of invasion from well-organized military powers. Ardrey knows this, for later on he tells us that France fell to the Germans because it had become a noyau. But again he misses the thrust and complexity of historic events. Would he venture to say that Holland, Denmark, and Norway were also noyau, or were they overwhelmed by German might for other reasons?

Individuals living in the noyau are highly emotional, enjoy their fights, but, nonetheless, lead a relatively relaxed existence. It is all done for fun and noyau people are happy-go-lucky. They are just like lepilemur!

The nation, on the other hand, is a *sodality*. It is made up of a group of individuals living in harmony but poised for battle with their neighbors. Thus "nations produce heroes, nouaux geniuses. The nation is anti genius since survival rests on uniformity of response." (*"Territorial Imperative,"* p. 184) The noyau is accepting of foreigners; the nation is suspicious.

The nation exists first in animal society. It consists of "a social group with at least two mature males holding a continuous space, which isolates itself from others of the same species through outward antagonism. Through defense of its territory the nation achieves leadership, cooperation, and a capacity for concerted action." (*Ibid.*, p. 191)

If one follows Ardrey's arguments it is irrelevant whether one is considering primates of one sort or another, the Bushman band, the Greek city state, or the United States of America. All are nations. It must come as a shock to most anthropologists that the Bushman band is a nation, for it is a group founded on kinship ties and not on allegiance to some territory. Furthermore, recent careful study of other hunting and gathering peoples has shown that such groups are rarely if ever territorial. Territoriality, when it occurs in human society, is a product of cultural evolution and not man's genes.

According to Ardrey, the nation provides security from predators in nonhuman species, but in man it acts as a defensive system against members of one's own species, members of other social groups. Human beings formed nations because of their physical vulnerability. It was a union of the weak providing strength through group action. A human group in possession of a social territory must behave according to Ardrey's laws of territoriality. Patriotism is an instinctive response, a part of the territorial imperative. It does not have to be learned, but is released automatically in response to certain sign stimuli. This notion is documented by Ardrey's own response to the attack by the Japanese on Pearl Harbor in 1941. He tells us that Americans all over the United States responded instantaneously to a challenge from the outside, and that patriotic commitments were made autonomously and in "silence." He says that this response was voluntary and that it was universal. In addition, it was contrary to personal interest. He admits that, for himself, until the moment of crisis he had a contempt for generals and the military. He says that certain words that had vanished from our vocabulary between the wars suddenly reappeared spontaneously. If we are to follow this logic, those individuals in our nation who were against the more recent war in Vietnam would appear to be a bunch of genetic freaks. For Ardrey feels that the surge of patriotism which occurred at the Japanese attack and which persisted during the war was a resurgence of the territorial instinct. The preparations for war, both material and psychological, the rules against treason which overnight silenced opponents, the real threat to lives as well as property, the existence of a draft law to insure an adequate army: all these are ignored in his analysis.

What is the function of territory? We have already been told that it serves to stimulate the pair bond and protect offspring. Along with the need to defend territories animals have learned (how does one learn an instinct?) that intrusion is unrewarding and therefore most territorial species avoid challenging each other's space. The degree of cohesion within a territorial species is a function of the degree of enmity occurring on the outside in the form of conspecific aggression and hazard (danger due to natural causes other than those brought about by members of one's own species). $A = E + h$ (Amity = Enmity + hazard). A lovely pseudo-formula, for nowhere is any attempt made to quantify it or test it rigorously. But Ardrey knows (instinctively?) that math is good science. In his view, amity is not natural, it must be made; only an outside threat can draw individuals together. Enmity *is* instinctive and can create its opposite. I agree that amity is not natural, but neither is enmity. The initial social experience of the infant and the reinforcing qualities of his later social life influence the future expression of amity and enmity. Among species, few are truly hostile, and among those which are, most, like the mink and weasel, are not at all social. For man, according to Ardrey, territoriality and the amity–enmity complex go together, although they need not do so in all species. The territorial principle for man has perfected the amity–enmity morality. It is supreme. Then comes the usual diversion. Without ever proving his case for primates, Ardrey leads us down the familiar path toward *some* of the lower animals. He tells us that three examples will suffice to show that the amity–enmity complex works in *other than primates* as well as in higher animals.

Ardrey notes that this basic fact of the human condition was seen by two early scientists, Herbert Spencer and his American disciple William Graham Sumner, but it slipped away under the liberal ethic and the insidious work of the behaviorist psychologists. But even Sumner and Spencer are chided by Ardrey, for neither fit into the instinct camp. Both (wrongly) felt that the amity–enmity complex was something particularly human and that it could be changed through the course of social evolution. This is no doubt true, for both men saw social evolution as a process distinct from (if related in principle) to the process of biological evolution. Both looked for social causes of social events. In short, they recognized certain facts about human behavior under specific types of so-

cial organization which they attempted to analyze, but they
never attributed such behavior to the function of instinct. In
spite of the fact that both Spencer and Sumner were arch-
conservatives, neither was pure enough for Ardrey. They
came close, however, and Ardrey assures us that they had no
followers because the virtues of "honesty, courage, and intellectual ruthlessness" are no longer admired. Only one fossil
remains among the scientists—Sir Arthur Keith, a man of Ardrey's own persuasion. For Keith the dual code was deeply
entrenched in human nature and had its roots in the animal
past, forming an inescapable part of man's history.

According to Ardrey, history is capable of temporarily di-
verting man's basic instinct but it can never submerge it.
Thus, the Jews, deprived of territory for generations, were
therefore unable to cope with antisemitism. Once restored to
the soil of Israel, however, their human nature reappeared
and with it the Jewish nation. The Sabra (native Israeli) is
different from the Jews of the gas chamber because he is no
longer deprived of his biological heritage. The Jew has discovered that nationhood is a far better solution than assimila-
tion. So strong is the tie to nationhood that it takes precedence over internal conflict, providing, of course, that the
threat from the outside is great enough to create internal solidarity. Although Ardrey's argument regarding Israel might
seduce some readers, its extension to other historical cases reveals its limitations. Ardrey believes (could it be wishful
thinking) that in South Africa the external threat has united
black and white men to pull together against the rest of the
continent.

Ardrey's own political morality becomes clear when he pre-
dicts that if South Africa were invaded by white forces 80
percent of all South African blacks would come to the coun-

try's defense. If black forces were to invade, 100 percent would rise to defend the country.

Realistically, the situation in South Africa is unique in the sense that revolution is difficult in a country in which topography provides few places to hide, in which political repression is total, and which has its borders protected by friendly states. Revolutions used to be fought with squirrel guns, but such weapons are of little use in the face of tanks and fighter planes manned by a people whose government sanctions the use of napalm and other antipersonnel weapons. It is likely that South African blacks do not revolt because they know that the only result can be a massacre of their own people. They have not forgotten the lesson of the Sharpeville riots and they know full well that their white "brothers" are ready to kill all of them, and themselves if necessary, to maintain the *status quo*. They know this because it has been told to them by the whites and because they have seen the South African government in action. The extraordinary repressive measures which the South African government has seen fit to impose upon black people demonstrates again that there is nothing inherent or automatic about territorial loyalty. It is something that has to be earned or, conversely, imposed on a population.

The last chapter of *The Territorial Imperative*, "The Three Faces of Janus," raises some interesting questions and backs away somewhat from the aggression–territory hypothesis. Here Ardrey sets three factors (identity, security, and stimulation) above the territorial instinct. Few social scientists will dispute this final section, although the biological necessity involved creates difficulties. Identity of self appears to have always been a human need. Security has always contributed to self-fulfillment, and stimulation, particularly in infancy, ap-

pears to be a major factor in unlocking man's genetic potential. There is some evidence that a lack of security fosters aggression and that identity models will also have an effect on a
wide range of behavior. Lack of stimulation leads to the
dulled response potential of the feral child. But Ardrey has
things upside down. He is not concerned with the process of
identity formation, with the type of identity engendered by
the enculturation process, nor with the choices available
within culture for security, choices which range from blind
obedience to the constant joy of stimulation and creativity. In
fact, the creative aspect of man apparently escapes him. Instead, he tells us that only two factors satisfy these three
needs at the same time, territoriality and aggression. There is
a kind of metaphysical economy in this: all three factors are
satisfied by one of two behaviors which are instinctual at
their base. But this in no way solves the human problem of
meeting these needs, nor does it help us to understand the
end product: social man.

# CHAPTER 4

# THE NAKED APE AND THE
# EMPEROR'S
# NEW CLOTHES

DESMOND MORRIS, the author of *The Naked Ape,* has an advantage over both Lorenz and Ardrey. He is well versed in evolutionary theory and knows his primates. When he talks about the evolution of human behavior and morphological development, and when he goes on to construct a theoretical protobehavioral system which might provide the basis for culture he is at his best. Morris displays a fertile imagination and is able to combine fact with speculation creatively. On the other hand, as we shall see, when Morris discusses culture he has a tendency to fall into the same clichés offered by Lorenz and Ardrey.

Morris sees the evolution of man as a process in which intragroup dynamics play a significant role. Thus, he sets his focus not only upon biological drives and their expression in outward antagonisms, but also upon the evolution of the social group, stressing both morphological and behavioral changes which would favor group cohesion. This is an important line of attack, for in addition to physical differences the human being may be separated from his primate cousins by his particular type of social group and his ability to communicate with fellow members of that group through language. Morris goes well beyond aggression and territoriality in his explanation of human behavior, concentrating, for example, upon creativity, a capacity which, when mentioned by the other authors at all, is taken as the root of human problems. Morris clearly does not subscribe, as do Lorenz and Ardrey, to the doctrine of original sin. He has his own set of myths, which appear to be derived from *The Emperor's New Clothes*. When he views man as nothing more than a naked ape he closes the door on the very essence of man, culture.

During the transition from ape to man a series of peculiar anatomical changes occurred, leading finally to such features as the large lip, expressive face, upright posture, large mammary glands, lack of body hair, bipedal gait, etc. Morris attempts to explain and integrate these traits with the behavioral prerequisites of a hunting society and with each other. He expresses a keen awareness that behavioral and morphological evolution are only separate aspects of the same process.

The loss of hair is related directly to man's hunting existence in a hot, relatively dry climate. When man is forced to chase game on foot, any mechanism which could increase body cooling would be beneficial to the species. The loss of body hair along with an increase of sweat glands serves this purpose well, but in order to conserve body heat under conditions of diurnal change (nights can be quite cold in the dry tropics) a subcutaneous layer of body fat was substituted for the fur coat of man's herbivore ancestors. The removal of insulation from the outside to the inside allowed for the development of an efficient air-conditioning system. The loss of hair, once selected for, could provide the added benefit of serving a communication and sexual function in a species in which touch and vision were more important than smell.

Morris notes that in contrast to other primates man is a highly sex-oriented animal. This observation rests not upon the works of Freud, but upon more recent sociological, psychological, and physiological data on courting, sexual anatomy, and the sexual act itself. (The reader might wish to consult *The Human Sexual Response* by Masters and Johnson.) He notes that humans take more time in courting and in sexual play than most species and that the sexual act itself is of long duration. The "sexiness" of man is subservient not to reproduction alone (for old primate patterns would suffice for this) but to the process of maintaining bonds between males and females which in turn, if they are stable, can help maintain group unity and reduce jealousy. Properly patterned sexual behavior can help to insure the continuity of the long dependency period of immature offspring as well as the continuity of the social group.

Morris' argument proceeds something like this: first of all, man had to hunt to survive. Man's hunting pattern included upright posture, which freed the hand for tool and weapon use. Furthermore, hunting for a physically weak species has to be a cooperative group activity. Brain power, expressed ultimately as culture, was substituted for physical strength. The bigger brain, however, required a longer maturation period and made infants and children dependent upon adult care for a long period. This led to a division of labor between hunting men and child-oriented females.

Morris fails to see an economic function of women in the division of labor which would strengthen his argument. In most hunting societies females provide a major portion of needed calories in the form of gathered vegetable products. This energy is used by men in the hunting process, which frequently consumes more calories than it provides. Hunting is necessary not for food bulk, but for its contribution of essential amino acids to the diet.

The maintenance of social stability in these hunting–gathering bands is enhanced by the development of a pairing tendency in females, increasing their faithfulness to their mates. On the other hand, weaker males in the group were needed in the cooperative hunting venture. Sexual rights had to be granted to these individuals. Sexual anarchy within the group would be reduced if males as well as females had a rather strong pairing tendency. Since the men were armed and therefore deadly, sexual rivalries could be extremely dangerous, and acceptance of the pairing bond would successfully reduce tension within the wider social group. Note that this idea runs counter to the aggression hypothesis in that Morris provides a mechanism which overcomes the facility to kill that comes with the invention of weapons. For Morris, the total evolutionary process leading to modern man is based upon the interaction of several strands of development. He is aware that a unidimensional view is unprofitable. Man is not a killer, because inhibiting mechanisms develop as part of the evolution of the social process. The tendency to aggression itself is seen not as an instinct but as a consequence of certain rivalries which had to be contained if the type of emergent social group was to be successful.

The ability to become "sexually imprinted" on a member of the opposite sex is thus a major step in the emergence of man. The pair bond is related to the dynamics of the family situation. The loss of a temporally long parental bond creates a relationship void that has to be filled. Once in love, man would have to stay in love, "making sex sexier keeps the bond going" (*The Naked Ape*, p. 65). Copulation in the human species helps to cement the pair bond. Although Morris ignores the frequency of polygyny or extramarital relations in human groups, what he says makes partial sense because polygyny in most cases is actually a luxury found primarily (and frequently) in technologically advanced cultures. Extramarital relations do not necessarily break the solidity of the pair bond, for marriage is frequently more a sociological union than a sexual union. Conversely, mating is not marriage, and copulation need not produce social union.

The concept of the pair bond is important to both Morris and Ardrey. But for Ardrey it results from territoriality and the amity-enmity complex while Morris relates it to sexual union and is part of a wider social complex. Ardrey and Lorenz see a total continuity between phylogenetically earlier forms of behavior and human behavior, while Morris searches for new combinations of the raw material imbedded in our biological heritage. This represents a fundamental difference in approach.

The hypothesis of heightened sexual needs makes sense out of a series of traits which are peculiarly human. Among these are the largest penis of any primate, the development of prominent lips, and full breasts. Morris suggests that these are signaling devices as well as erotic zones in a species which spends much of its time in face-to-face confrontations. This is related also to the development of the verbal signal system, language. Morris points out: "Virtually all of the sexual signals and erogenous zones are on the front of the body" (*The Naked Ape*, p. 73). Heightened sexuality in *Homo sapiens* includes the development of the female orgasm, for which no evidence exists in lower species. Morris suggests that orgasm has the double virtue of increasing sexual pleasure for females and facilitating the movement of the sperm towards the egg by keeping the spent female on her back for longer than would otherwise be the case. This might be important because humans as a bipedal species have the problem of gravity working against conception.

Morris does not deny the importance of territory in the dynamic of group formation, but he does not see territoriality as an instinct. It is rather the outcome of the sexual dynamic. As soon as the offspring begin to mature they become sexual rivals. They may then be driven out of the group. They will also begin to develop a need for a "territory" of their own. The phenomenon of exogamy (marriage out of the group) must have developed biologically or "the typical breeding system of the species could never have emerged from its primate background" (*The Naked Ape*, p. 81).

Such an analysis puts Morris on the threshold of an important insight, but he never takes the final step. This would be to grasp the dynamic of selection for the human species: a process both biological and cultural in which those populations which as units had developed more efficient technological systems could out-reproduce other groups. Living in relative isolation, most hunting groups were (and are) small and widely scattered. Efficient populations would expand naturally and then divide. These smaller groups would then prop-

agate both their genes and their culture without direct competition or aggressive interaction. From time to time,
particularly with mounting increases in population, contact
would occur allowing for both genetic and cultural exchange.
The development of society based on culture would allow tal-
ented individuals to contribute to the well-being of the entire
group. Under these conditions, in which solidarity benefits all
individuals and protects the social group as a whole, altruism
could develop out of the cooperative aspects of group life.
Such altruism and the capacity for empathy (a specifically
human trait) would be the product of internal family socialization, the extension of the pair bond downward to offspring
and upward toward parents. The extension of kin ties to
other more distant relatives and finally to friendly strangers
would not be difficult, but neither would it be instinctive or
automatic. What I am saying is that the dynamic of successful social existence creates its own environmental pressures
which then act to shape and reinforce what were originally
more or less patterned biological trends. This is a process
which begins long before the appearance of primates, but
which is elaborated in social primates. It finds its full fruition
in man. The capacity to use language and culture adds an
important dimension to social and technological innovation.

Human behavior and the development of culture cannot be
wholly explained on the basis of heightened sexuality combined with the hunting pattern. Morris sees two important
drives which when properly balanced lead to a successful
cultural adaptation. These are the need to imitate and the
need to explore.

Morris considers music, dance, and plastic art to be mani-
festations of an explorative drive and drives a series of interesting rules governing such behavior. 1. Investigate the unfa-

miliar until it has become familiar. 2. Impose rhythmic repetition on the familiar. 3. Vary this repetition in as many ways as possible. 4. Select the most satisfying of these variations and develop them at the expense of others. 5. Combine and recombine these variations with one another. 6. Do this all for its own sake, as an end in itself.

The social psychologist Omar Khayyam Moore has come to similar conclusions about game playing activity, which he sees as a nonpunitive way of learning one's culture. The reward comes from the act of playing itself and the play situation is a protected substitute for the real world and its hazards. Artistic behavior is included by Moore as the form of game playing in which the individual experimentally manipulates his environment.

Alfred Kroeber among other anthropologists has suggested that artistic play leads to technological innovation. And both Morris and Arthur Koestler as well as the present author have noted a similarity between scientific and artistic exploration. Moore has successfully applied his theory, which has the formidable title of autotelic folk models, to the teaching process. He has developed a machine based on the electric typewriter with which three- and four-year-olds can be taught first to type and then to read. As in all teaching machines (like those developed by the psychologist B. F. Skinner, for example), the learning process is reinforced by the successful act of learning itself. The reward comes from winning the game. An interesting combination of programmed learning and game playing has been developed as Wiff-n-Proof, a logic game invented by Layman E. Allen at Yale University. In Wiff-n-Proof the players move through a series of games which increase in complexity with developing skill. The speed and ease of learning obtained with such games tend to support the theory that game playing has its role in the learning process. The expression of a capacity for exploratory behavior is, of course, determined by individual genetic factors, socialization, and cultural factors. The exploratory element in game playing and/or its imitative aspect can be heightened or dampened by the rules set by particular cultures.

Morris also notes that boredom, stress, and social isolation, the hallmarks of a zoo existence, create behavioral ritualization in animals which stands in contrast to their behavior in the wild. Thus, he is aware of the important effects of interpersonal stimulation upon animals including man. He warns us that man has created a human zoo.

Morris says that animals fight either to establish social hierarchies or to establish territorial rights, and that in some instances fighting serves both goals. But he also points out that predatory killing, that is, hunting, does not automatically imply aggressive (intraspecific) killing. He also argues against the idea that man has an inborn urge to kill his opponents. An animal wishes to defeat its adversary in order to dominate it, not kill it.

> What has happened, however, is that because of the vicious combination of attack remoteness and group cooperativeness, the original goal has become blurred for the individual involved in fighting. They attack now more to support their comrades, rather than to dominate their enemies and their inherent susceptibility to direct appeasement is given little or no chance to express itself. (*The Naked Ape*, p. 176)

These are important and perhaps valid points. It must be stressed, however, that while the analysis is sufficient to describe a part of what happens in war it provides no explanation of the causes of war. Morris' inability to separate the dynamics of warfare as they touch on individual behavior from its causes leads him to a one-sided view of the world's problems, and he sees massive depopulation as the only sound solution.

One need only look at the Vietnam war to see that it is not a conflict based on an overpopulated nation's thirst for territory. The whole problem of expanding markets and the relationship between industrial and underdeveloped countries, as well as rivalries between great power blocks, is overlooked.

In regard to religion, Morris cleaves rather closely to the classic Freudian approach. God is the father and symbolizes man's submission. Authority itself is the result of unequal power within the social group. God comes to represent leadership and supports the secular authority. Morris believes that the tendency to submit to a powerful member of the group is inherited from the subhuman primates, some of whom function in rather large hierarchically arranged social units.

A look at the data from comparative religion would suggest a more multifaceted approach, one which would combine the projective aspect of religion with man's symbol-making ability and his need to account for the unknown. Culture itself tends to generate a search process, some of which finds its outlet in religious energy. Such rules have an ordering function and render the behavior of members of one's own society predictable. It is only one step from social rules which find expression in society to rules about the operation of the universe which "explain" phenomenon not yet explained in everyday or scientific terms. Religious systems frequently appear to be a projection of the existing order. Morris is right, I think, when he sees God as a representative of the leader in societies which are based on one or another type of leadership principle. But this is not universal. One need only look at the amorphous nature of Buddhism to see how far religions can diverge from Morris' simple formula.

Religious ritual does not necessarily involve subservience to God but it does involve repetitive acts. It would seem, therefore, that religion serves both the need to explore and the need to imitate. The imitative aspect of religion serves a useful purpose for it is a major source of education for the young and serves to preserve a set of culturally validated symbols.

There is also a creative, sometimes artistic, side to religious behavior manifested, for example, in the search for philosophical transcendance. Those philosophical systems which have rejected empirical reality have frequently done so within the context of a religious movement. Those philosophies which have not been part of organized religion have often arisen as a response to it, but not within the realm of science, quite apart from it. Thus, Jaspers finds much in common between the thought of Kierkegaard and Nietzsche, although the former operated from the context of Christianity, and the latter attacked religion. Even Nietzsche searched for some transcendent quality in man.

It may be true that certain behavioral trends which man inherits from the primates find their outlet in religion, but in sum religion is particularly immune to biological analysis. It is the product of culture and the symbolic mode of thinking. Only man is capable of asking the question, what am I?

As we have already seen, Morris sees territoriality operating in the service of spacing. From this he derives the hypothesis that one of the important features of such territory is that it must be easily distinguished from all others. Its location makes it unique, but this is not adequate. Its appearance must also make it obvious and easily identifiable so that it can become the personalized property of the occupiers. He extends this basic hypothesis to a discussion of the discordance between modern crowded urban housing and our animal nature, suggesting that the drab sameness of it all can create psychological damage. Unfortunately, he links these psychological problems to the loss of territory created by the zoo-like nature of housing projects. If such housing does in fact create psychological damage, might this damage be due not so much to difficulty in identifying one's territory (after all, if this were necessary other symbols could be easily substituted for the house itself) as to the sameness which limits stimulation? It seems to me that Morris makes a good point about the function of stimulation (both social and esthetic) in his comparison of urban life with the depressingly standard second-rate zoo. Why invoke a dubious territorial need? Spacing in man does not seem to be a major problem as long as enough land exists for necessary economic activities. In addition, what is crowded for individuals accustomed to one demographic and cultural situation might appear to be open space to others accustomed to a different set of conditions. This fact was brought home to me when a friend of mine from Calcutta remarked that New York City was so empty.

Morris stresses the fact that man evolved while living in small hunting bands in which population density was always extremely low and in which face-to-face interactions were therefore restricted to a few individuals. This is true, but we can only wonder at the amazing accommodation man has made (obviously with little genetic change) to the urban condition. Morris himself offers one clue to this problem when he remarks that we have developed anticontact behavior with which we manage to keep the number of people with whom we interact on an intimate basis down to an optimal minimum. What we do is create small "tribal" groups out of our circle of interactions.

Surely if we were still nothing more than naked apes we would be unable to erect the kind of cultural defense which Morris describes. The ability to weed out significant others from the mass of daily contacts represents one triumph of culture. This, of course, is the key to an understanding of the interaction process which occurs between biology and culture. The capacity for culture is biological; the problems of adaptation which human populations face are also biological, but the responses made by humans are largely cultural.

Morris' major weakness appears in his discussion of the food quest. He attempts to maintain the nakedness of the naked ape at the expense of greater insight into the workings of human behavior. Morris reduces the argument to absurd generalizations by suggesting that *because* modern agriculture has left males in our society without a hunting role they compensate for this by going out to work. Like hunting working involves a regular trip from the home base to the "hunting" ground. Risk taking and planning are part of work as they were part of hunting. "The Pseudo-hunter speaks of 'making a killing in the city,' he becomes ruthless in his dealings. He is said to be 'bringing home the bacon.'" (*The Naked Ape*, p. 188) Such an analysis puts Morris in the ranks of those who substitute metaphor for science. But worse, he loses sight of the different attitudes held toward work in different cultures and even within cultures. Thus, in our own society he ignores the service professions and the attitudes of many of our citizens toward work as a satisfying occupation

in which the basic goal is the amelioration of human misery
or the formation of good citizens (good within the accepted
cultural pattern). He loses sight, also, of the reasons for the
cynical attitude toward work justifiably held by so many who
see themselves as victims of the need to earn money in jobs
which carry little or no satisfaction. In these cases work is a
pursuit of money necessary to feed the family, but it has no
other function in the life of the individual. In our own industrial system in which so much work is of a dull or routine
nature even the middle-class professional often structures his
life around a series of culturally prescribed leisure activities
which are supposed to relieve the boredom of everyday existence. But, as we know, the malaise is not always overcome.
Morris ignores the whole economic structure of society, of
market relationships, of industrialism and capital investment,
and the psychological effects which these economic relationships have upon those who are embedded in the system but
who can do nothing to change it. He is blithely unaware of
those societies (excluding the "exotic tribes" he chooses to ignore) in which the compulsion to work, to "make a killing" is
far less an important aspect of culture than in Western nations, and he ignores the historical changes which have occurred in economic relationships in the course of our own history. To reduce economics to the food quest and the food
quest to "basic biological principles" is to obscure any understanding of man *qua* man.

Among animals who adapt largely through learning, curiosity itself has a tremendous survival value. It helps in the
hunting process because a good hunter must learn about the
terrain on which he hunts and must understand the behavior
of those game animals on which he depends. His learning
cannot stop there. The more an individual knows about his

environment the better he can control or manipulate it. This process of exploration and learning, and not specifically hunting, has been the history of humanity from the beginning of our existence.

Morris continues his process of *reductio ad absurdum* when he draws an analogy between grooming talk, the cosmetic industry, dress customs, etc. and the physical process of social grooming seen in our primate cousins. Here again, however, I think he does make a contribution to an understanding of the dynamics of human behavior. Body care is certainly one way of maintaining social unity. A mother training her offspring to wash and dress properly does more than instruct. She interacts physically with her children in an intimate way and contributes to the formation of the first social bond within the context of the family.

Dress patterns, which are conditioned by cultural rules, serve as a complex set of signaling devices which expand the nonverbal vocabulary beyond our mere physical differences and similarities. Clothes are often used to heighten the natural sexual dimorphism which exists between males and females. They are also, however, signals of class, ethnic, and at times religious membership. They help to define the ingroup but at the same time serve to mark one group off from another. Thus, dress patterns and grooming rules are related to an important set of secondary social bonds which reinforce the sociality without which we could not survive as individuals. Many of the primates, man among them, are social animals, and human society has been built upon certain animal patterns which worked before the advent of man. Pointing these out helps to provide a basis, a beginning, for the understanding of man.

Morris ends his tale where anthropology begins, yet he re-

jects anthropology. On pages 9 and 10 of *The Naked Ape* he
tells us:

> One of the strangest features of previous studies of Naked-Ape
> behavior is they have nearly always avoided the obvious. The
> earlier anthropologists rushed off to all kinds of unlikely cor-
> ners of the world in order to unravel the basic truth about our
> nature, scattering to remote cultural backwaters so atypical
> and unsuccessful that they are nearly extinct. They then re-
> turned with startling facts about the bizarre mating customs,
> strange kinship systems, or weird ritual procedures of these
> tribes, and used this material as though it were of central im-
> portance to the behavior of our species as a whole. The work
> done by these investigators was, of course, extremely interest-
> ing and valuable in showing what can happen when a group
> of Naked-Apes becomes sidetracked into a cultural blind alley.
> It revealed just how far from the normal our behavior patterns
> can stray without a complete social collapse. What it did not
> tell us was anything about the typical behavior of typical Na-
> ked-Apes. This can only be done by examining the common
> behavior patterns that are shared by all the ordinary success-
> ful members of the major cultures—the main stream speci-
> mens who together represent the vast majority. Biologically
> this is the only sound approach.

The language here is certainly not calculated to produce
understanding, for a scientific investigation of "bizarre mating
customs, weird ritual procedures, and strange kinship systems" shows that they are subject to the same scientific laws
which determine our own set of beliefs and customs which
are neither more nor less bizarre than the customs of primitive man. Anthropologists have not spent years away from the
comfort, both physical and mental, of their own culture, just
to document insignificant distortions of the "normal" pattern
of human existence. As humanists, it is true, anthropologists
have cataloged the customs of the world's dying peoples to

preserve the richness of the human condition, but as scientists they have had other goals. First and foremost among these has been to demonstrate once and for all that major behavioral differences among the world's people are due to culture and not biology. This work has gone a long way in destroying the racial myths which guided European and American thinking about human nature since the time of early exploration. Second, anthropologists have frequently demonstrated that behavioral systems other than our own can be understood in terms of accommodation to local environmental conditions. It is a form of biological adaptation which is freed of the rigidity of the genetic code. Third, anthropology has gone far afield to test a range of behavioral hypotheses because they cannot be tested within the confines of our own social structure. We are not free to manipulate the lives of individuals, and the range of laboratory experiments which are possible is limited by moral and humanist considerations. Field work operates as a substitute for the laboratory, for it is possible to discover human groups who live under conditions which accommodate to experimental needs. They provide a natural laboratory for the testing of hypotheses concerning relationships between economic behavior and religion, between kinship systems and family structure, between family structure and economics, etc. Certain socialization practices present anthropologists and comparative psychologists with the opportunity to test hypotheses which link infant training with adult personality and with such cultural projective systems as religion and ritual. The comparison of a range of societies living under variable environmental conditions allows us to search for rules of social development, and a comparison of different technological levels helps us to unravel the complicated relationships which exist between economics and the rest of the social system. To do this effectively one cannot enter the field with any preconceived notions about the weirdness of systems other than our own. Nor can we assume that our own cultural solutions are the best under all possible conditions and for all the world's peoples.

# CHAPTER 5

# TERRITORIALITY AND AGGRESSION REVISITED

THE REALITIES CONCERNING aggression and territoriality in human groups are far more complicated and interesting than the interpretations of Lorenz, Ardrey, or even Morris suggest. This complexity emerges with the unfolding of human capacities within the context of the bio-social environment. Human beings must accommodate themselves to their natural setting just like any other species. This is done, however, largely through the creation of cultural systems which, although limited by physical factors and genetic potentials, are not determined by them. As these cultural systems develop out of human action they create their own restrictions, limiting and shaping the direction of change. Such systems have a ten-

dency toward stability, but nonetheless they are always in the
process of change. Conservative forces are balanced by innovation. Contradictions within the system which produce in-
stability, and variations in the environment, tend to stimulate
change. In addition, few, if any, social groups exist in
isolation, and there is a constant interplay among different
cultural systems which involves exchange of information and
culturally induced environmental change. The manipulation
of the environment by one group may have consequences for
the behavioral systems of groups in the immediate or even
somewhat distant social environment even when such groups
have little contact.

In this chapter I shall present and analyze data from my
own field work among the Abron people of the Ivory Coast,
where one of my major research concerns was how aggressive
behavior develops and is channeled in a society which
overtly shuns aggressive action, but which nonetheless trains
its children in such a way that aggressive behavior is likely to
find some outlet, some expression in behavior. The patterning
of aggression makes sense only in the context of the socialization process and the structure of Abron society. Attitudes toward territory and possession as manifested in property holding and inheritance rules as well as a pattern of residence in
which husband and wives live apart also demonstrate how far
afield from strictly biological patterning we must go in order
to understand the operation of human society. Among the
Abron the facts of property are tied to the expression of aggression but in ways which no biologist could predict on the
basis of instinct theory.

In what is to follow, Abron social patterns and responses to
these patterns will appear to be more uniform than those in
our own society. I must caution that such uniformity has both

real and unreal aspects. Anthropologists intentionally choose to study societies more uniform than our own, in order to limit the range of interfering variables. Most Abron share a common set of beliefs, although a few of them have been converted to Islam or Christianity (less than one percent are Catholic, about one percent are Moslem, and Protestant conversions during my field work counted less than fifteen individuals). Abron bring their children up according to social rules which are common to most of their fellows. The economic system is relatively egalitarian and almost all Abron do the same thing to make a living. And although change is occurring, the system was coherent enough in 1961–62 for me to make rather broad generalizations about Abron social life. This is not to say that the system was stable or unaffected by the larger cultural context of the Ivory Coast or a world economic system in which the Abron play a small part. As growers of coffee and cocoa, Abron farmers are tied to an economic system over which they have little control but which affects them in direct and indirect ways. Some of the changes brought about by the development of private property make up part of the story.

Anthropological analysis abstracts patterns from individual units of behavior produced by actors who share a common tradition but who nonetheless differ considerably in personal characteristics. These individual differences are lost in the analysis which follows, for it was my task to factor out those which were irrelevant for the problems I chose to analyze. The reader then must be warned that the impression of uniformity is forced upon him by the anthropologist. It is a partial artifact of both the focus of the study and the interpretations which I have imposed upon the data. Flesh and blood Abron are as real as we, and as complex individually as each of us. It is only their social system which is simpler, and by simpler I merely mean more uniform.

The Abron constitute an ethnic group of about 10,000 people organized as a state under the authority of a king and a hierarchy of district and village chiefs. Questions of government are settled, however, on every level with the assistance of a council of elders (usually male, but including some females, particularly very old women). They live approximately 250 miles north of the Atlantic Ocean along the Ghana border. Their territory is located in the zone of transition from tropical forest to savannah, or grassland, and is marked by large, relatively open fields of tall grass interspersed with palmettos. This pattern is occasionally broken by forests in low-lying areas. Culturally, the Abron are related to the large Akan speaking group of Ghana and the eastern Ivory Coast which includes such ethnic groups as the Agni, Ashanti, and Baoule. Although they no longer speak an Akan language they are, like their neighbors, matrilineal (inheritance of property, membership in social groups, and succession to office descend in the female line from a man's eldest sister to her eldest son). The Abron live in the so-called yam belt of West Africa and indeed their major subsistence crop is the yam, a plant which should not be confused with the sweet potato (called yam in the United States). It is a long tuber, varying in color and size, depending upon species, and tastes very much like an ordinary potato. Yam gardens must be carefully weeded. The vines which grow from the developing tubers must be tied on supporting poles or young trees.

Historically, the Abron are closely related to the Brong of Ghana and are, in fact, classified as Brong by many anthropologists. Sometime in the seventeenth or eighteenth century Akan tribes in what is now Ghana formed a confederacy

which grew into the Ashanti Empire. Local tribes in the area
had to choose between joining the confederacy, fighting it, or
migrating from the territory. Those Abron who are today
known as Brong joined the confederacy and constitute a part
of Ashanti. These Brong speak Twi, the local Akan language.
Another part of the Brong fled the expanding Ashanti Empire
and moved westward into the territory of unrelated people,
the Kolongo; these are the Abron of today. According to tradition, the Abron conquered a segment of the Kolongo people, but it is my impression based on existing social patterns,
that they merely moved in on them. Today the two ethnic
groups occupy the same area of the Ivory Coast and because
they speak the same language, Kolongo, and share many social patterns, it is difficult to distinguish individuals as Kolongo or Abron.

The Kolongo have no political unit higher than the village
presided over by a chief. Since population density is low in
the area, it was not difficult for the Abron to penetrate the
territory and take up residence in the empty spaces. Soon
their superior political organization involving a central authority was imposed, at least partially, on those Kolongo
among whom they lived. Today there are villages which are
known to the people as pure Abron, those which are known
as pure Kolongo, and those which are mixed.

The interpenetration of territory is not a rare phenomenon
in the area or in other parts of Africa, for that matter. The
largest town in what is technically Abron country is inhab-
ited by a patrilineal, Islamic, non-Akan speaking people from
the west of the Ivory Coast. These people, the Dioula, are
traders and have lived in peace in the area for several
hundred years. To the north, in "pure Kolongo" country not
under the political control of the Abron king, one finds sev-

eral ethnic groups. Some of these are closely related; others
follow life styles which are divergent from either the Akan or
Kolongo pattern. None of these tribes are as politically cohesive as the Abron and there is no question of one being dominant over any other. Not only do they live in harmony, but
they are partially dependent upon one another in a rather
complex local economic network.

Evidence that the Abron moved peacefully into Kolongo
territory can be found in the system of land tenure as it affects the two groups. Villages as units are said to hold land.
Abron villages own their land in common and Kolongo villages theirs. Title may pass to individual kinship groups (li-
neages) if they are resident in the village, but such title is
based on use, that is, to be retained the land must be worked.
Strangers coming to live in a village must obtain permission
of the chief and the village elders to use open land. This is
usually granted and there is no shortage of savannah on
which subsistence crops are grown. Forest, however, is relatively scarce and valuable. This has been true at least since
the introduction of the cash crops, coffee and cocoa, both of
which must be grown in shaded areas. (These crops diffused
from the east before intensive European contact.) The Abron
recognize that forests belong to the Kolongo and by their
own rules must ask permission of Kolongo to work it. Once
granted, such permission is permanent. In addition, mineral
rights are held by the Kolongo, and the extraction of gold
also depends upon Kolongo permission. This is a strange kind
of territoriality indeed. And it is not a new pattern imposed
upon the people by Europeans, for such land tenure patterns
are documented in the 1920s before European domination.

Abron villages range in size from about ninety people to
several hundred. Individual residence is with the same sexed

parent; that is, women remain in their mothers' houses and men with their fathers. This is true even after marriage. Such a pattern, known in the anthropological literature as duo-local because married couples live apart, is quite rare although it does occur in other parts of the world. As we shall see below, the exotic nature of this residence pattern, far from being irrelevant to our understanding of human behavior, provides a test of a hypothesis concerning aggressive behavior. How does this residence affect individuals? Let me begin with a marriage. As I have already stated, the married couple stays apart. The man is in residence with his father (or in some cases with his maternal uncle). The male household consists of men related through a female line (a man, his full brothers—children of the same mother—and their sons, who are related to each other only through their fathers. The woman lives in the house of her mother and her mother's sisters, with her siblings and the children of her mother's sisters. This household is different in structure from the men's house in that all the females are related in the same female line. Put another way, several kin groups are represented in the men's house because a boy inherits his kin group from his mother rather than his father, but only one kin group is represented in the women's house, since all the females are related through the same female line. Parallel residence (patrilocal for men and matrilocal for women) produces different social situations for men and women. This is an important point and I shall return to it later.

When the couple has children they stay with the mother until weaning, which occurs at about thirteen to fifteen months. The Abron have a rule that a woman may not have sexual relations with her husband from the birth of a child until it walks. This spaces pregnancies and can and, in this case, does serve to prolong the nursing period. Nursing may continue a few months into a pregnancy if the woman's fertility has returned during nursing. Although the belief exists in our own culture that women who nurse are infertile, this is not always the case. After weaning, boys join their fathers in the men's house. Girls remain in their mother's house.

The Abron are polygynous. If a man has two or more wives, they will live in different houses, since a man is not permitted to marry sisters. This creates a convenient situation and the Abron themselves are aware that such residence reduces (but does not eliminate) quarrels between wives of the same man. As in most polygynous societies the sex ratio is about equal. Polygynous marriages are fairly rare and tend to occur for a man in his later years. Many young men remain single for a considerable period, since marriage involves the payment of a rather high bride price.

Unlike a woman, a man cannot stay in his house for life since it belongs in reality to a female line other than his own. On the death of the last surviving senior male of the same kin group related through a line of women (the last of the full brothers) it passes on to the eldest son of the eldest sister of these men. This follows the standard inheritance pattern of the Abron which, as I have already indicated, is matrilineal (from man to man through a line of related women). The pattern of inheritance extends to land holding as well. A man does not inherit from his father but from his maternal uncle. This does not mean that relations between fathers and sons are distant, however. As if often the case, especially in matrilineal societies, fathers and sons are very close. In many such societies the maternal uncle is occupied with the discipline and the father is free to play a supportive role. But among the Abron, because the son usually lives with the father, he is also disciplined by him. Since he is a member of his father's household (a viable economic unit) the son works with his father and shares the father's economic resources rather than those of his own matrilineage. But the son cannot inherit from his father. In former times when all property was held by groups of kin and when there was a relatively equal distribution of economic resources (the system was based on subsistence with no private property and no cash crops) few social problems were associated with such a system. The disjunction between residence and inheritance did not cause great difficulties. Any male could expect to shift his economic allegiance from his father to the group of his maternal uncle without a loss of wealth. At present this situation no longer holds. Private land holdings in the form of coffee and cocoa plantations exist and wealth is unequally distributed. A man may work hard for his father only to see the fruits of his labor pass on to his maternal cousin and he may inherit little from his uncle. Conversely, of course, a man may have a poor father, but a rich uncle. Women may also hold property in private under the new system but the strains between residence and inheritance do not exist. A woman lives and works with her mother and she also inherits from her mother (if she is the eldest daughter; if she is a younger daughter she inherits from her older sister, but this does not change the situation). For women the residence group is the same as the inheritance group. There is no disjunction. Splits and jealousies which occur among men should not occur among women.

Let me leave this pattern for a moment and pass on to the system of child training and socialization. Later I shall show how these two aspects of Abron culture lead to particular results.

The Abron love children. A newborn baby is the center of

its parents' affection, and it is frequently fondled by all adults, but particularly by the members of the two concerned households. Babies are fed on demand and sleep on either their mother's or older sister's back during the day or next to the mother in her house at night. There is a great deal of social and physical contact between the baby and its relatives and it is very definitely a center of attraction. Parents are very indulgent and not punitive. Toilet training is late, mainly because the Abron use deep pit latrines placed some distance from the village, which would present a considerable danger to young children. Weaning, on the other hand, is fairly abrupt. Mothers usually put pepper or some other bitter substance on their breasts and feed their child with mashed yam.

Shortly after the weaning period the mother may become pregnant again. As soon as a baby is born the previous child is replaced in the affection of the parents. This is not to say that the child is any less loved, but overt attention is now turned toward the new child. Most babies who have been quite placid up to this point begin to show signs of rage and aggression. Rather than being an automatic response, it appears to be the result of the displacement process. The child is frustrated in its attempts to attract attention and to continue close physical contact. Its care is now in the hands of older siblings or other related children who treat it with a great deal more indifference than it had been accustomed to. Abron society is heavily age ranked and older individuals, even children, expect a great deal of deference from those younger than themselves. Younger children perform simple tasks for their elders and give up both food and comforts as well. In addition, the newly weaned child may suffer nutritional deprivation since its major food source is now starch.

While obvious Kwashiorkor (protein malnutrition) is rare among the Abron, since even children get some protein in the form of beans, and older children get both meat and fish, the very young child may suffer a short period of subclinical protein malnutrition which may produce a further physiologically based irritability. Older children and adults do not react with indifference to this irritability. Aggressive behavior is punished sometimes with such fury that I was led to the conclusion that such overreactions were themselves a form of aggression which under normal circumstances is repressed. Children who fight are immediately punished by adults; the victim as well as the instigator. I remember vividly a case in which a mother attacked her daughter, who had been fighting, with such violence that the girl cowered under her mother's blows for a good fifteen minutes. But the violence was tempered. The mother heaped verbal abuse on her daughter and kept throwing a half eaten orange at her. The fury and the embarrassment were real but, interestingly enough, the physical punishment was light. The orange had been drained of its juice and could not really hurt the girl. Harder blows do occasionally fall upon children but for much shorter durations. The children are intimidated by this punishment, but not physically hurt, yet the parent appears to overreact to the situation.

Interestingly, aggression is quite generally the only form of behavior which is so severely punished. The only other transgression which appears to be considered serious by adults is lack of respect for elders and such a lack of respect itself can be interpreted as a form of aggression. The result of such training, and training it is, is the almost total repression of overt physical aggression. But it does not disappear. Abron society has developed a range of socially sanctioned outlets for aggression which allow its expression in disguised form. Some of these forms tend to maintain the solidity of the social group and so, as in animals, aggression can serve a social function. But not the same way as in animal society. Except for some minor outlets which I shall describe briefly, aggression is turned against imaginary beings, witches, rather than against living members of the social group.

First, the minor outlets. One of these, the overpunishment of children, has already been mentioned. There are two others. Abron children frequently torture animals, particularly small creatures such as insects and birds. On more than one occasion I saw young children pull the wings off live birds, and older children as well as adults often tease or abuse dogs and cats in various ways. This is a case in which agressive feelings are directed onto another species. In addition, the Abron delight in other people's minor misfortunes. Serious injuries are reacted to with concern and empathy but if someone has a minor accident, everyone will laugh. If the accident is the result of some clumsiness the laughter is all the more mirthful. Once I saw a whole group of adult men watching a young boy learning to ride a bicycle. They waited for him to fall off and when he finally did everyone laughed.

Abron adults, particularly women, frequently argue, and while voices are raised and threats hastily thrown, people almost never come to blows. Sometimes gestures are made which indicate violence. But this occurs only when someone is close enough to restrain the actor so that it will look as if he or she was about to initiate a fight. Face is saved; violence is avoided.

Most Abron and other Akan peoples with whom I have had contact also enjoy what I call a game of strategy. It consists of attempting to fool someone or refusing some information.

If, for example, you want to know what time it is and ask an Abron wearing a watch the likely response is, "Why do you want to know?" If you respond that you have an appointment, you will be told that you should get a watch. All this is done lightheartedly and, as soon as the questioner departs, laughter is general. I found this behavior extremely annoying in the initial days of field work, but adjusted to it. Later I found out that I too could play, and that my efforts would be appreciated even by my victims. One day when I was visiting a village in which an Abron friend had told me an important god has his temple, I had the opportunity to test the joking situation. The village chief and all the people of the village denied the existence of the god. The next morning I got up early and set out on my own to find the shrine. I discovered it after a short search. I then went to the chief and asked him if he could tell me the name of the god I had discovered. He said that he could only do that with the concurrence of the village elders since I was a stranger and "European". I already knew the name, but asked him if he would ask the elders to decide. He agreed, and they were called in from the fields where they had already gone to labor. It was quite hot and some of the fields were far from the village. It took some time for the men to come in. They arrived rather hot and tired and out of sorts. The chief then described the problem to them and they deliberated for about one half hour while I sat silently listening to the argument. The question was not trivial since most Americans they had had contact with were missionaries and therefore enemies of their own god. I had, I thought, convinced them of my distinctiveness from the missionaries but the question was clearly still open. Finally I indicated to the chief that, in fact, I really did know the name of the god, and revealed it to the assembled group. Fortunately I had the correct name. Far from raising their anger, the fact that I had fooled them sent the elders into gales of laughter. Even from their point of view the pain I had caused was worth the result, for not only had I scored a strategic point, but I had demonstrated that I knew the rules of the game.

These outlets for aggression are minor. The greatest amount of aggressive behavior is displayed against witches. In Abron society this is the perfect outlet because, in fact, there are no witches. Let me explain. The Abron religious system is based upon a hierarchy of deities with the high god or creator at the top. This god, Nyame, has little to do with the affairs of men and can be reached only through the intercession of intermediate gods. These range in scope from a deity for Akan peoples down through village gods to family and in some cases individual deities. All such lesser supernatural entities are known as *gbawkaw*. The cult of these *gbawkaw* is celebrated by priests or *kaparese* (pl. *kaparasogo*). Gods protect the lives of individuals or they may be asked to do personal favors. When this is the case, the individual concerned must enter into a contractual relationship with the particular *gbawkaw* in question. The supernatural world is also peopled by ancestors whose spirits must be supplicated and the ghosts of nonrelatives. Ancestors never harm their relatives except when they themselves have been offended or when, lonely in the land of the dead, they kill a relative to provide themselves with company. Basically the *gbawkaw* and ancestors are good supernatural entities. They may do good and when they harm someone it is usually to punish him. Evil spirits exist also. Among these are the ghosts of nonrelatives who may occasionally annoy the living, forest and water spirits who trick wayward individuals but who are relatively benign, and bush devils who are truly dangerous.

Between the natural and supernatural stand the witches (*derese;* pl. *deresogo*). These are human beings who have inherited specific qualities from other witches. They have inborn supernatural qualities such as the ability to change themselves into animals, to fly, to become invisible, and to kill from afar. It is important to stress that these abilities cannot be learned. One is either born a witch or one is not. Thus the *deresogo* contrast with a group of mortals which I shall refer to as sorcerers. These individuals, usually of Moslem faith, know both black and white magic and employ it for good or evil, depending upon the situation. These sorcerers may be hired to cure a sick individual in place of a *kparese* or they may be employed to kill or injure an enemy. To reiterate, sorcery is a profession, witchery is a gift. Sorcerers do not always advertise themselves but they do exist in the social system and when in need they can be found. No one ever finds a witch or at least not until the witch is already dead.

The Abron are very concerned about the cause of death and they want to know if a dead person was a witch in his lifetime. Before every funeral except that of a baby, the corpse is asked a series of questions, some of which will determine its fate. This is done in the following manner. A bit of skin from the genital area, some hair from the head, and nail clippings are placed in a small cloth sack. This sack is then placed on three or four poles supported horizontally on the heads of two village youths. The young men march forward balancing these poles on their heads. A questioner then asks a series of yes or no questions. The first one is always "Were you a witch?" If the answer is no the poles remain balanced and the questions go on to determine the reason for death, eliminating one possible cause after another. After this, the funeral rites proper commence. On the other hand, if the corpse admits to witchcraft (the poles gyrate and almost fall off the heads of the bearers), the body is immediately cast out and left for the vultures to eat. Thus, the villagers are able to avenge themselves on the evil one who has lived in their midst. Aggression against witches is usually carried out in this manner. If, however, many people in a village have died suddenly and if the dead report that they were murdered by witches the villagers will take action against living witches in the community. A special ceremony for this purpose is convened and a non-Abron diviner is employed to point out who the witch is. While all male adult villagers participate in the ceremony they are never the ones to stigmatize the witch. The scapegoat is always chosen by an outsider. Once found, the witch is either killed or driven from the village. In this case the villagers are guilty of aggression against one of their members, but they are not responsible for naming the victim.

Priests claim to know all the *deresogo* in the village and they will act to protect individuals against witchcraft, but they will never reveal who the witches are. Among the several *kparesogo* I interviewed, all told me that the *deresogo* were very powerful and that revealing them would be dangerous. During field work I became interested in the Abrons' attitude toward strangers and city life. Among other things I wanted to know if they feared living away from their own villages and their own kin. I therefore asked them if they would fear attacks from witches living in their own small village, in a larger and ethnically mixed trading town, or in Abidjan, the Capital of the Ivory Coast, a city of close to 200,000 people. I expected most people to express a fear of the city. In all cases people admitted that they most feared witches in their own village. I then discovered that a peculiar feature of Abron witches is that they can only harm individuals in their own family. If a witch wants to harm someone who is unrelated to him he must ask one of his fellows to perform the task. In general, individual Abron fear witches in their own kin groups.

My interpretation of these data is that a good deal of the hostility and aggression that is fostered during the socialization process finds its outlet through the mechanism which Freud named "projection." Since individuals fear to express or even feel aggression in themselves they project it onto others. Feelings against aggression are so strong, however, that it would be difficult to admit that other normal people had such feelings. Thus, it is only witches who can be aggressive. They must be punished but aggression, even against them, is dangerous. The Abron, therefore, punish only dead witches or hire a non-Abron to find the living witches for them. Aggressive feelings arise out of the family situation, particularly the displacement of children by the newborn; they are actively repressed through the socialization process in which aggressive displays are punished severely. Individuals fear members of their own kin group most, for it is towards their relatives that they felt their first aggression, and it is their own kin who have punished them, often unfairly. It is interesting that among the related Ashanti people witches are feared only in one's own matrilineal kin group. Among the Abron, on the other hand, bilateral kin (mother's or father's side) are all potential witches. This change may have occurred with a shift in residence patterns (the Ashanti are only temporarily duolocal) and the development of private property.

After I had discovered the relationship between fear of witches and social structure I was able to run a further test on the hypothesis that strains in the social system were responsible for the particular pattern witchcraft took in Abron society. If the reader will remember, there is a disharmony between inheritance and residence for men but not for women in Abron society. I therefore expected to find differences in attitudes towards witchcraft among men and women. I asked a sample of men and women why witches kill. In most cases the men replied that it was over jealousy concerning property. This jealousy is complicated and amplified by the fact that, while inheritance is matrilineal a man can, in his lifetime, give gifts of property to his own sons. Men may wish to kill their uncles before such gifts have been made, insuring that they will have eventual title to their uncles' property. Women agreed that witches kill out of jealousy, but the reasons for this jealousy were different. Most women told me that if a woman has too many children, particularly girls, a witch in her family might kill her out of spite. The factor of jealousy is constant for the two sexes, but the reasons behind this jealousy rest upon differences in the social situation as it applies to men and women.

The process of analysis here began with the collection of data in a society with social variables considerably different from our own. As more data were collected, a coherent picture began to emerge which allowed for a theoretical interpretation. The theory itself was tested in part through the collection of more data. This time I knew what to look for and the process of fitting the pieces together became easier. As it turned out, the additional data fit the theory. It was possible to predict, if not in detail, what kind of effect the split in Abron social structure would have upon witchcraft beliefs. More important, however, was the support such a prediction gave to the general hypothesis that the phenomenon of witchcraft in Abron society rested upon familial tensions. What the data does not prove or disprove, however, is my general theoretical position that ultimately witchcraft results from the projection of aggression onto others, that these others cannot be humans (since the Abron cannot admit the existence of aggression in the community of normal individuals), and that the generation of aggressive feelings and their later suppression is a product of socialization. I think that such a theory makes good sense and it has the virtue of accounting for and linking together a set of phenomena, but one must always bear in mind that such a theoretical superstructure is difficult to establish empirically. Further testing of the general hypothesis could have been carried out through the use of projective tests corrected for use in the field situation. I regret at this point that I did not, in fact, employ such testing devices. Another method of testing the theory, or at least the constancy or predictability of concurrence between sets of variables, in this case certain socialization procedures and a set of social outcomes, would be to employ the method of cross-cultural analysis. This method involves the comparison of data on a set of societies in which the independent variable (a particular kind of socialization process) is known to occur. The researcher sets out to find positive correlations between such an independent variable and the dependent variables, in this case the generation of aggression and its suppression with subsequent projection. Incidentally, the theory as it stands does not predict what form the projection will take beyond the fact that in cases of severe suppression the projection should be directed towards either some supernatural or quasi-supernatural beings or towards members of some socially defined outgroup. I have not gone beyond the original analysis of Abron society, primarily because my interests have since turned elsewhere, but I mention these methods to illustrate in a more concrete way why anthropologists gather data on "exotic" tribes in far-off places.

It is, I think, worth mentioning here that a study of witch-craft among the Navajo Indians published in 1944 by Clyde Kluckhohn shows striking parallels and some differences be-tween Abron and Navajo witchcraft. Kluckhohn offers data to support the hypothesis that Navajo witchcraft is related to the projection of aggressive feelings onto others. Among the Navajo, however, most witchcraft accusations involve strang-ers rather than members of the family, although these strang-ers are almost invariably other Navajo. In addition, under in-creasing deprivation there is a tendency toward an increase in witchcraft accusations even directed toward relatives. Kluckhohn raises the question of ingroup vs. outgroup witch-craft and says:

> The problem of out-group versus in-group witchcraft is, how-ever, much more complicated than this. The primary determi-nant is probably: which form is more congenial to the major cultural configurations or the single integrating principle. . . . Thus the Mountain Arapesh's attributing *all* witchcraft to alien groups seems to fit the general plot of that culture. (Kluckhohn, *Navajo Witchcraft*, p. 97)

The important factor here is that witchcraft, when it oc-curs, appears to operate in similar ways in different societies and that differences may be attributed to cultural (and I would add ecological) factors.

The reader will note in this short description of Abron cul-ture that territoriality and aggression are both manifested in ways which no biological theory could predict. The Abron, one segment of a larger ethnic group, refused to join a more powerful political entity and moved into the territory of an-other people. I have suggested but I have not proved that this was a migration carried out peacefully. I have indicated, however, that the peaceful interpenetration of territory is a fact in part of Africa. In addition, land tenure relationships between Abron and Kolongo indicate that certain culturally defined territorial rights are respected on both sides, but that these in no way correspond to what we see in subhuman animal communities. Furthermore, intermarriage between the two groups through time has tended to blur the ethnic distinctions. The Abron speak Kolongo as a first language and are more like these people than like their ethnic brothers, the Brong of Ghana. As far as aggression is concerned, it appears to occur as a response to specific conditions and a specific time in the life stream of individuals, when permissiveness and indulgence are rudely disturbed by the appearance of a new infant within the family. The impulses of the child for gratification are blocked but so are its responses to this blockage. This situation is a far cry from the rather automatic and highly patterned aggressive responses which occur in lower animals under specific sign stimuli. Interestingly, however, aggression in Abron society, if my explanation of it is correct, does serve the function of maintaining group unity. For it sets the normal community against the abnormal witch. Since witches are real only in a social-psychological sense, the normal individuals in the community are drawn closer together. The similarity here between the function of aggression in many animal societies, particularly those which are territorial, is based on entirely different processes, however, and in the Abron case it has nothing to do with social spacing. Witchcraft beliefs are the result of the symbolic process which itself is based upon learning. The entire dynamic that is entailed in this set of beliefs and actions is purely cultural.

My colleague, Andrew P. Vayda, has suggested that witchcraft might under certain conditions also function as a spacing mechanism. There is evidence from other parts of Africa that increases in the activity of witches lead to a breakup of the community and population dispersal. Tensions in the crowded community (crowded remains to be defined) lead to witchcraft accusations and the fear of supernatural attack. The best means of avoiding such attack is to move away. The objective manifestation of witchcraft activity might be an increase in disease incidence or crop failure, both of which can be the direct and objective outcome of overcrowding. The hypothesis has the virtue of providing a link between the biological needs of the community and a cultural response to them. This hypothesis is testable, although it involves a longitudinal study of a type rarely carried out by anthropologists. If the hypothesis is correct, it would demonstrate how cultural mechanism can be substituted for purely biological ones in the process of adaptation.

Humans are not immune to the problem of biological adaptation which faces all species and they cannot be removed from the realm of evolution. But the recognition of a set of biological bases in human adaptation does not demand that solutions depend upon the action of instincts. On the contrary, human environments, both physical and social, change too rapidly for successful solutions to be based on stereotyped instincts. The cultural solution is much more economical and flexible. This does not mean that genetic processes are nonoperant in adaptation. But such processes do not add up to changes in instinctual patterning. Rather, they may affect behavioral capacities as they certainly did in the evolution of *Homo sapiens*. The manipulation of the environment through culture creates new selective pressures on populations; genetic structure may be altered accordingly. Conversely, new genetic patterns, which occur through the process of random mutation may increase the ability of a population to exploit a particular type of environment. A hypothesis of this sort has been offered by Weisenfeld ("Sickle Cell Trait in Human and Cultural Evolution") concerning the incidence of the abnormal hemoglobin gene in West Africa. The occurrence of this gene in malarial areas protects its carriers from the disease and therefore allows populations carrying it to live in disease-ridden zones. The ecology of the mosquito which carries Falciparum malaria is related to man's effect on the environment since the mosquito breeds only in sunlit pools. Thus the opening of the forest cover increases the danger of disease, which can only be overcome by populations which adapt genetically to these culturally created conditions.

Anthropologists have noted that technologically primitive societies, particularly hunters and gatherers, have been pushed into environmentally isolated corners of the world usually unfit for agricultural exploitation. Unable to compete with technologically advanced peoples and outnumbered by them (in most cases agriculture can support larger populations than hunting and gathering) these ethnic groups have either become absorbed or have been forced to retreat to refuge areas deep in the forest or desert. In many cases those groups which have survived show an amazingly uniform tendency to avoid aggression. While this state of affairs may have come about through the conscious realization that aggression could only result in annihilation, it may also be the result of selective factors favoring *cultural* solutions in which the avoidance of conflict would have been the only successful strategy for survival. As we shall see, such avoidance of aggression is not a biological trait, but yet another cultural accommodation to reality. The fact, too, that the societies in question depend upon hunting contradicts the hypothesis that predation and aggression are related phenomena. The pygmies of the Ituri forest, as I have already pointed out, are extremely successful hunters but they are also unaggressive in their relations with other pygmy groups and with the Bantu peoples on whom they depend for such items as salt, most carbohydrates, and iron.

Not only are such groups nonaggressive but they are also nonterritorial. Different pygmy bands meet each other in the course of migrations and hunting through the forest, but such meetings do not produce antagonistic encounters and groups do not see themselves as attached to particular spots.

Perhaps the most interesting and direct study of nonaggressive behavior is that carried out by Robert Dentan among the Semai of Malaya. Dentan spent well over a year with these people and was overwhelmed by the emphasis on nonviolence in their culture.

The Semai live in the hills and mountains of central Malaya. They are a small group of slash and burn agriculturists who have recently given up a hunting and gathering existence (although they still hunt) and have retreated under pressure of the more culturally advanced Malays. According to Dentan, they number about 12,000. While the Semai hunt, they also raise some domestic animals, particularly chicken. "Traditionally, no Semai would kill an animal he had raised, but would exchange it with a person in another village, knowing that that person would kill the animal. . . . The buyers are usually Malay or Chinese traders." (*The Semai*, p. 33) Unlike the Abron, the Semai are not cruel to these animals. "The Semai talk and whistle to tame birds and they fondle chicks. They behave yet more affectionately to four-footed pets. They adopt young animals as eagerly as they adopt children, fondle them as they fondle children, address them as "children", give them names, and even suckle them. . . . Pets are rarely sold and never eaten." (*The Semai*, p. 34)

Interpersonal relations among the Semai are focused around the concept of *punan*.

> Implicit in Semai thinking about *punan* is the idea that to make someone unhappy, especially by frustrating his desires, will increase the probability of his having an accident that will injure him physically. The word *punan* refers to both the offending act and the resulting accident proneness. The Semai say that *punan* accidents result somehow from the fact that the *punan* victim's heart is "unhappy". A Semai who has had an accident, like barking his shin, will often blame the accident on *punan*, due, for example, to his wanting something he could not get." (*The Semai*, p. 55)

As Dentan points out, the concept of *punan* is particularly interesting because the punishment affects the victim and not the committer of some social breach. For *punan* to work, it follows that the Semai are not the sort of people who would do each other physical harm.

The Semai are conscious of this and refer to themselves as a nonviolent people. According to Dentan, the Semai say that anger is bad and that, in fact, they rarely get mad. An angry man (they do, after all, get angry) will deny his anger. "The point here is not that sometimes individual Semai violate the nonviolent image, for they do, being human. It is, rather, that they continue to conceive of themselves as nonviolent." (*The Semai*, p. 56) This nonviolent image is consistently applied by Semai and non-Semai alike, and they are known in Malaya as an extremely timid people. As Dentan points out, however, Semai life is not without conflict. When an individual is offended, he may endure the resulting *punan* or he may ask compensation from the individual who has offended him. The most frequent cases in which *punan* is *endured* occur when a man is refused the sexual favors of a woman.

Compensation will be granted when an individual admits that he has offended someone. This does not always occur, and quarrels may develop. These are sometimes adjudicated by disinterested individuals but frequently none can be found and the dispute simmers for some time. Its expression in open hostility and aggressive action is almost always limited, however, to insults and the spreading of rumor. Sometimes a Semai will start throwing his own property around, but he is careful not to hurt anyone. Even so, such behavior is frowned upon because it scares people. Dentan further notes that drunken Semai (drunkenness is rare in Semai society) do not display a personality reversal in which open hostility and aggression are displayed. In addition, unlike the Abron, the Semai never hit their children. They fear that such hitting might cause physical damage. The taboo on hitting is extended to adults as well. "Some idea of the horror that physical violence inspires in Semai is revealed by the fact that when east Semai are talking Malay they translate the Semai word for 'hit' as 'kill'." (*The Semai*, p. 58)

It is not surprising that murder does not occur in this culture and in fact not a single case has ever come to the attention of the authorities.

Semai child training is similar in many ways to that of the Abron. Permissiveness is the general rule but coddling and intensive fondling of infants ends rather abruptly after they walk. While children are not punished physically, they are made to fear transgression of behavioral norms. (This is probably a significant difference in the child training procedure.) Strangers, evil spirits, and certain natural phenomena, such as storms, cause fear in adults which is readily transmitted to children.

> During a storm, the adults cry, "Fear! Fear!" to the children and urge them to cover their eyes against the lightning and their ears against the thunder. The adults thus increase the children's own fears of the violence of nature. The next time the children seem to be becoming noisy and potentially losing their self-control, the cry of "*tarlaid*" recalls to them the terrifying thundersquall and subtly suggests to them that the expression of human violence would be as devastating as the storm. The children in this way apparently learn to fear their own aggressive impulses. (*The Semai,* p. 60)

Unlike the Abron, the Semai do not punish aggression in children. They rarely see violence even as a punishment for the transgression of the moral code. Children are unable to rebel against their parents since the parent is unlikely to respond. When children fight they are snatched up and taken away from the scene of the battle. Dentan concludes: "The absence of punishment means that the would-be aggressive child has no model to imitate, and that, not knowing for sure what the results of human violence are, he winds up with an exaggerated impression of them." (*The Semai,* p. 61)

During the communist rebellion in the 1950s, many Semai joined the military. Since they had a negative reputation as fighters no one thought they would make good soldiers. Dentan suggests that they were initially lured into service by wages, and various material items, and that they did not realize that a soldier's function is to kill people.

> Interestingly enough they were wrong. Communist terrorists had killed the kinsmen of some of the Semai counterinsurgency troops. Taken out of their nonviolent society and ordered to kill, they seem to have been swept up in a sort of insanity which they call "blood drunkenness." A typical

veteran's story runs like this. "We killed, killed, killed. The
Malays would stop and go through people's pockets and take
their watches and money. We did not think of watches or
money. We thought only of killing. Wah, truly we were drunk
with blood." One man even told how he had drunk the blood
of a man he had killed. Talking about these experiences, the
Semai seem bemused, not displeased that they were such
good soldiers, but unable to account for their behavior. It is
almost as if they had shut the experience off in a separate
compartment, away from the even routine of their lives. Back
in Semai society they seem as gentle and afraid of violence as
anyone else. (*The Semai*, pp. 58–59)

I suspect that there may be an element of exaggeration in
the Semai's reportage of their behavior in battle, for war and
killing form such a sharp contrast with both their experience
and their morality. On the other hand, there is no doubt that
they were not only able soldiers but were caught up in the
bloodshed. Now, how shall this be interpreted? Ardrey and
Lorenz would no doubt suggest that their natural instinct was
freed of cultural restraints, that their true nature which had
been hidden for so long was finally free to express itself. Such
a response begs the question. Under their own rule system
the Semai developed a nonviolent culture. In addition, the
fact that the Semai could be violent in another context shows
that their usual nonviolence was not the result of genetic
selection as might be suggested. It would appear reasonable
that the potential for aggressive action was there and that it
was expressed when stimulated by external cues. The Semai
fear strangers and appear to project aggressive feelings outside of their community much as the Abron do. This would
make it easier for them to alter their behavior under a new
set of circumstances. Unlike the Abron, the Semai do not ag-
gress even against supernatural beings in their midst. This

device which serves the Abron so well has probably not developed within the Semai cultural system because children are not punished for aggression and because the social tensions which exist in Semai culture are very different from those which the Abron experience.

It must be stressed that we have been discussing aggression and not war in this chapter. The causes of war, why people fight, and why certain groups are more successful as warriors, are related to aggression only in the sense that under the proper environmental conditions human beings are capable of aggressive action. The action itself may be set off, however, by the cold, unaggressive calculation of individuals within a society's power structure, or by the force of a particular historical circumstance. Lest the statement sound metaphysical, let me turn in the next chapter to an analysis of warfare patterns among the Iroquois, who in the early days of the American colonies and during the Revolution emerged as a strong military confederacy and who have been the subject of many myths concerning their own warlike nature.

# CHAPTER 6

# ON WAR

LET ME BEGIN by defining war as armed conflict among socially defined groups of human beings. I shall leave aside for
the moment a discussion of differences between "primitive
and modern war." Note, however, that the "groups" in question can be highly variable (social definitions may change
radically in a short time) and that the conflict itself has a social basis. That is to say, when such conflict occurs it is
human beings who define the membership of antagonistic
groups. In certain technologically primitive societies it is the
locus of the dispute which determines the size and constitution of warring groups. When society is structured by sets of
increasingly larger segments of relatives descended from a
real or fictive common ancestor, for example, as in much of
Africa, fighting can occur between like units. A fight between
brothers is a strictly personal affair, for they are members of

the same social segment. A fight between cousins, on the other hand, if it persists, will lead to the mobilization of sets of brothers occupying different segments. The more distant the kin in the dispute, the larger the number of individuals who may be mobilized on each side. This extends beyond tribal boundaries so that if a dispute breaks out between men of different ethnic groups they may be able to muster their entire social unit behind them. Units as units may also conflict on any of these levels.

The goals of warfare differ from group to group and from situation to situation. Recent documents (such as Chagnon's *Yanomamo*, 1968) show that in very primitive societies territory is rarely, if ever, a cause of war. The reasons for hostile action may include raids for females, personal disputes between individuals, including minor insults, and resource distribution. Groups, particularly those with more advanced technologies, may fight to gain access to scarce goods. The more advanced the technology, the greater the diversity of goods and the greater the likelihood of shortage in some areas. Shortages need not be overcome through conflict, however, and one must not minimize the ability of humans to make trading arrangements which tie a set of social groups into an economic network. Such a network may or may not reduce warfare, for the causes of war are not always strictly economic. The frequency of personal feuds and wider social conflicts may be determined by demographic and other ecological factors which are tied to problems of adaptation, such as overcrowding, rather than to any existing need for raw materials or manufactured goods. There are social arrangements which allow trade to continue in relative peace even in the midst of war. Trading with the enemy is not foreign even to our own political system.

Certain important differences between human war and conflict between members of the same infrahuman species are readily apparent. Among nonhuman species the conflicting groups are relatively stable. The social network, once established, is quite permanent and in-group fighting is rarely serious. Lorenz is quite correct in pointing out that such conflict serves to stabilize the social structure and reduce both disorganization and potential loss through physical violence. He is also quite correct in pointing out that inter-group hostility is often ritualized, acting to define geographic and social boundaries, and again to reduce the possibility of real violence. It is Lorenz' lack of awareness that this picture does not fit human groups which leads him astray. For while he admits differences of result (human war is usually highly destructive), he fails to see that the causes of human conflict are not the same as those which operate in animal society. His emphasis remains psychological and his sociology is primarily dependent upon hypothetical mechanisms which compel individuals toward aggressive action. Thus for him war is merely aggression gone astray. The role of culture has been to upset a biological balance; it has a negative but no real adaptive function.

Human war, of course, can be quite serious, but interestingly enough, it is rarely so in primitive society. This is not because weapons are simple (primitive hunting peoples could annihilate each other if they chose to do so) but rather because the motivations for war, which are partially psychological and partially social, are generally of an order quite different from that in modern society.

In contrast to man, animals can reduce conflict through ritualized aggression but they cannot form inter-group alliances. Nor can they in most cases, incorporate groups producing new alignments. While they do not frequently kill one another, they are also incapable of making peace. Antagonism must smolder continuously, for if it did not aggression could not serve its various adaptive functions.

In human society aggression is often mobilized, even created, to fit a war which is planned by certain interested segments. Those who plan a war need not feel aggressive toward their enemy, although they *may* feel aggressive (partially a defense mechanism). And, of course, humans may fight defensively or may be led to believe that they are doing so. Animals cannot be fooled because they have no culture. Humans can be led astray by the very symbolic process which is their major adaptive tool.

Elman Service has pointed out that most anthropological descriptions of primitive warfare have been limited to ethnic groups which have been strongly influenced by the incursions of foreign, particularly Western, culture. Warfare patterns in these groups cannot be understood without reference to the colonial situation. An examination of such a complex pattern of interaction, however, provides evidence against the simple Ardrey-Lorenz explanations of warfare. One of the best documented of these studies is that of George T. Hunt, whose *The Wars of the Iroquois* represents a careful analysis of those historical and social factors which lay at the root of Iroquois power. By placing these successes in their proper historical perspective, Hunt eliminates a tendency for their exaggeration, and goes a long way toward disproving hypotheses about war which rest upon biological factors alone. His study is so unusual in anthropology, and so important to an understanding of "tribal" warfare, that I urge you to read it.

The entire development of Iroquois military power is seen by Hunt in the context of the fur trade and relations between eastern tribes with the Dutch (later the English) and French as well as with each other. The introduction of trade goods (steel axes, guns, and traps, as well as other metal tools) which the Indians immediately realized were superior to their own manufactured items created a desire which soon turned into necessity as indigenous techniques were rapidly forgotten. The only resource which the Indians of the Northeast could give to the Europeans was fur. Hunting, trapping, and trading required an immense effort. The unit value of fur was set by the Europeans and enormous quantities of fur had to be delivered. This required a reorganization of tribal economies and led in some cases to the abandonment of traditional subsistence techniques. Hunting produced furs, but those tribes which could act as middle men, collecting pelts from a wider geographic area than they themselves controlled, could be richer and more secure than mere hunting peoples.

In some instances, particularly in the case of the Iroquois, trading grew in importance as fur-bearing animals in their own territory became scarce. Between 1626 and 1633 the Iroquois trade in beaver and otter skins skyrocketed. In 1626, 7,250 beaver and 800 otter skins were traded to the Dutch. In 1628 the number of beaver pelts rose to 10,000 and according to Hunt's estimates the number was nearer 30,000. By 1640 the animal reserves were exhausted. During this time the much more numerous and powerful Huron tribe controlled a vast trading territory to the north and west, containing more beaver than any other area in the world. Even before European contact, it would appear that the Huron were expanding and that the victim of their growth was the Iroquois.

The Iroquois, particularly the Mohawks who had been the

major trading partners of the Dutch, controlled only the region of the Hudson valley, but from that vantage point they were able to block Dutch access to other hunting peoples. When their own resources were depleted, they attempted to make commercial treaties with the French Indians, particularly the Huron. These attempts failed to materialize partially, at least, because the French themselves had no desire to see their trade slipping into Dutch hands. Jesuit priests played an important role in keeping the tribes from forming viable trade relations which could have been used to seize partial control of the trade network and thereby produce more favorable pricing conditions.

The Huron's empire was enormous, although it exerted no actual political control. "They gathered up and delivered to the French at Three Rivers and Montreal the entire accumulation of furs of an immense territory, reaching from the Sagueny and Lake Saint John on the east to Lake Nipigian on the west and from Lake Erie to James Bay." (Hunt, *Wars of the Iroquois,* p. 53) "The fall of the Hurons, the rise to affluence and power of the Ottawa, the depopulation of the western Ontario and Michigan and the repopulation of Wisconsin, the conquest of Pennsylvania and Ohio—all these were the results of the efforts of the Five Nations to get furs and assume the position held by the Hurons before 1649." (Hunt, p. 54)

The Huron position was exceptional. They were able to trade agricultural products of economically captive tribes as well as manufactured goods which they themselves produced (fishing nets, birch bark, nettle collars) for furs to the west, and then exchange these furs with the French. Their almost total dependence on trade, or the manufacture of trade goods, however, led to a diminuation of their own primary produc-

tive capacities. As long as the trade worked they were not
only safe but prosperous; a failure of trade, however, would
lead to early disaster. In short, the Huron had become overly
specialized.

The Iroquois, no greater in number than 12,000 or so, became directly competitive with the Huron primarily because
of their dependence upon fur, and the exhaustion of natural
resources within their own territory. In order to survive they
had either to make treaties with the Huron for a portion of
the trade or to conquer them. Between 1633 and 1640 the Iroquois attempted on several occasions to make treaties with
the Huron, but on each occasion the French were successful
in preventing the establishment of peaceful relations. In fact,
according to Hunt, priests who were particularly successful in
creating hostilities between tribes were praised by the French
secular authorities. By 1641 the Iroquois were in particularly
"strained circumstances". In that year they sought peace with
the French but were rejected. In 1642 they made war
against the Huron and in 1643 they intensified this war,
annihilating Huron parties in Iroquois territory; by 1644
they had managed to close the St. Lawrence River as
far up as Quebec. In 1645 the French attempted to make
peace with the Mohawks but the upper Iroquois were not
party to the treaty. This treaty was kept by the Mohawks
until the fall of 1646. The renewed outbreak of war was the
direct outcome of economic threat to the Iroquois, who saw a
great fur fleet coming to Montreal from Huronia and who
were unable to obtain any skins for their own trading.

The Huron at this time remained confident, since they had
over a year's supply of goods, the result of their own successful trading with the French. At the same time they made a
political attempt to disrupt the Iroquois by suing for a sepa-

rate peace with the Onondaga tribe of the confederation, which was joined by the Cayuga. This move was countered by the Mohawk and Seneca who in 1647 sent a large force to break communications between the Huron and the Onondaga. In 1648 trade was still good and the Huron managed to hold their own, but the real Iroquois push began in 1649. A large group of warriors fell upon the town of St. Ignace at night and only three Huron escaped to St. Louis. St. Louis was itself assaulted by the Iroquois the next morning. A few days later, probably unaware of the extent of their victory, the Iroquois retreated.

Although these battles produced no clear-cut military victory and relatively light losses for the Huron, the latter became terrified and disorganized. "Their security had vanished —the unexpected had happened." By that spring many Huron villages were abandoned and six to eight thousand fled to the now crowded Christian Island.

"By spring the Island was a place of horror, containing a few hundred Hurons who were little more than skeletons and who had for the most part survived only by practicing cannibalism." (Hunt, p. 94) Losses were as high as 10,000. In June of that year the Huron began a retreat to Quebec, some went to other tribes, and a large segment joined the Erie. The Seneca and Mohawk now moved into the vacuum. They dispersed the weaker Neutrals and Petuns. Trade rather than conquest was still the goal of these wars, however, and the Seneca sued for peace with the French in 1653. The Mohawks were not particularly satisfied at this time for they feared that the Western Iroquois would maintain a trade advantage with the French.

In fact the Iroquois had not succeeded in taking over control of the fur trade, part of which passed to the Erie. The latter tribe was destroyed in 1654 but the Ottawa who successfully mounted fur brigades from the far northwest were the real problem. In 1656 the Iroquois attempted to destroy them but were unsuccessful. Although their victories over both the Huron and Erie as well as some of the smaller tribal groups had led to a domino effect which produced the wide dispersal of several ethnic groups farther west, the Iroquois were never able to attain their economic goals. In the 1660s they suffered a series of reverses due to disease, battle loss, and the incursion on their own flanks of the Susquehanna. The so-called unity of the League was an idealized vision developed by such investigators as Lewis Henry Morgan, whose contact with the Iroquois nation was extensive, but dated from the middle of the nineteenth century. In fact at the time of major Iroquois success the political organization was never unified and the six nations were unable to act in unison.

Hunt's analysis shows three things rather clearly. First of all, the defeat of the Huron was due more to their own overspecialization as traders and manufacturers than to the military prowess of the Iroquois. Second, the Iroquois themselves sought war only when economic necessity forced it upon them. Far from being "warlike," they were sensitive to economic conditions and their own problems of survival. Remember that by the time of the great wars the Iroquois had already depleted the game in their own territory. Warfare was used to accomplish economic goals when other means failed. Finally, any supposed genetic superiority of the Iroquois in warfare or any inherent "innate fury" (in Leachman's phrase) attributed to them was clearly nonsense. They won some battles and lost others. They engaged in combat with genetically related peoples and success or failure depended upon social and environmental conditions.

It is also clear that a full understanding of the Iroquois case rests upon a wider historical analysis which includes the role of European governments in the colonial situation. Europeans themselves were in competition for natural resources and their dealings with local ethnic groups and each other had the effect of creating new political alliances, new feuds, and even, in many cases, the restructuring of indigenous social systems. This situation, far from being unique, was, and in many cases still is, the pattern over much of the world. As Elman Service has recently suggested:

> It should now be emphasized that the changes among the societies that experienced the worldwide increase in warfare caused by the spread of the Western nations were vastly more drastic responses. The increase in true warfare . . . was so great that even among egalitarian tribal and band societies the political-military consequences ranged from the formation of unprecedentedly great confederacies to refugeeism and downright extinction. The modern ethnographic record that we use in comparative studies is wildly skewed for these reasons (and for others as well, of course, especially because of depopulation due to European diseases). ("War and Our Contemporary Ancestors," p. 161)

The point Service makes is that warfare as we know it, even when it occurs among "primitive" groups, is conditioned by the facts of Western culture including economic exploitation and expansionism, as well as a set of new socioeconomic conditions created by the contact situation. Organization for war, the reasons for fighting, and the methods used are all taken as a special case dependent upon cultural and historical factors rather than on some inherent set of biological demands. The case may be extended to the operation of nation states such as China, but not to what has so loosely been defined as warfare even at the beginning of this chapter. Fighting between socially defined groups of human beings is dependent upon different motivations under different historical conditions. Generalizations about war as such tell us nothing about the causes of human action or its possible effects on the populations concerned.

If the case of the Iroquois shows how, under certain social circumstances, an entire group can turn to the practice of warfare, the case of Northern China shows how a single ethnically undifferentiated people can split into two cultural groups: one based on settled agriculture and the other based on nomadism, raiding, and war. This historical process is well documented by Owen Lattimore in his book *Inner Asian Frontiers of China* (1951).

Lattimore contrasts the natural setting of China north and south of the great wall. In the south where water was abundant agriculture became intense and came to support very dense settled populations. In the north, on the other hand, water was a scarce resource. Except for scattered oases agriculture was impossible. In order to survive in this environment men took to herding and a nomadic life.

> Change from intensive agriculture meant a relatively wide dispersal of the population and a loosening of the methods of administration that had become standard. Moreover, the lack of irrigation activity meant the dropping out of what early became and always remained an essential link in the chain of economic, social, and political control. (p. 41)

Lattimore places great emphasis on a difference between the use of horses in war and for travel: that is to say, between harnessed horses and ridden horses. He also emphasizes the differences between stall fed and pasture fed animals. In the latter case as horses become important elements in the econ-

omy and grow in number herds must be moved frequently
from pasture to pasture during the yearly cycle.

It was only when this diverging specialization had been carried to a certain point that the marginal steppe society ceased
to be marginal and committed itself definitely to the steppe.
Having reached this point it was ready to take advantage of a
steppe technique of horse usage in order to increase the efficiency of life within the steppe environment. (p. 59)

The standard of wealth and social importance became dependent upon steppe resources. This involved control over
large territories and great mobility to insure adequate pastur-
age.

The probable order of progression was: 1) abandonment of
marginal culture and transition to a culture of clearly steppe
character; 2) complete dependence of all livestock on grazing
. . . ; 3) greater need of movement, in order not to stay in exhausted pastures; 4) the particular need for a higher degree of
skill in the control of horses—because the average farmer who
has always tethered or stabled his horses and fed them with
grain and hay has difficulty in recapturing them if he turns
them loose on open grassy plains; 5) the acquisition, conse-
quently, of marked skill in riding and in the control of loose
herds of horses. (p. 63)

Military techniques evolved along with this shift in herding. Warriors, who formerly had fought on foot, became
horsemen on the treeless plain. Their battle techniques involved the development of a sturdy, short bow which could
be shot from horseback and the invention of the stirrup,
which increased the effectiveness of the mounted archer.

The Chinese to the south also took to mounted warfare, but
never subordinated their agriculture to nomadism. Their
horses and warriors remained inferior to those of the plains-

men except in abnormal periods involving long wars when professional cavalries were recruited.

On the steppe the demand for freedom to move increased the power of tribal lords who could regulate the distribution of pasture and migration cycles. This led to tribal wars which played their part in the maintenance of an effective system through a constant adjustment of claims.

As surplus stock accumulated, great chiefs looked south to China. If she was weak they raided her; if she was strong they increased trade and thus widened the social differentiation between themselves and the common people.

China is not the only place in which the horse played an important role in the transformation of relatively peaceful people to a war and raiding existence. Plains Indian culture in the United States became possible only with the introduction of the horse. The tall tough grasses which grew on the high plains made agriculture difficult and the lack of rapid means of pursuit made the alternate subsistence technique, bison killing on a mass scale, impossible. Indian culture was quick to adapt to the plains environment as soon as the means were available. The introduction of the horse led to the development of mobile groups in which bravery in hunting and war (which involved the capture of horses) became major elements of culture. The adaptation which involved a shift towards warfare and predatory patterns was cultural and not genetic.

Taking another tack, Andrew P. Vayda made a series of suggestions concerning the possible functions of war for various peoples in specific environmental circumstances. He has suggested that, in general, war might be a response to disturbances of an adapted, stable, behavioral system, and that it might function to restore such a system to stability. Disturbances may include restriction of access to economic resources or population increase which place strains on the existing economic system. In addition:

> Another hypothesis in the study of primitive war is a hypothesis of deterrence or "preventive war". According to this, warfare undertaken by a group to avenge an insult, theft, non-payment of bride-price, abduction, rape, poaching, trespass, wounding, killing, or some other offense committed against its members deters members of other groups from committing further offenses. (Vayda, "Hypotheses about Functions of War," p. 87)

Vayda also proposes hypotheses about the function of primitive war in the regulation of such psychological variables as anxiety and hostility. These are not tied to some automatic need to experience aggression, but rather to psychological conditions created by the social and ecological setting of warring societies. Nor would Vayda deny that solutions other than warfare could be employed to satisfy these conditions. War is a solution among other possible solutions.

In sum, war follows rules, but these rules are social and highly variable. War may be triggered by specific circumstances defined by changes in the environment and by the cultural system under stress. What solution will be found for what problem is the result of a complex of behavioral rules, many of which are founded on tradition and not genetics. The capacity for aggression which exists in humans can be mobilized for warfare. Whether or not it will be turned into active warfare depends upon historical circumstances involving rules of behavior, and what can be seen as recognized or covert threats to the system.

While warfare is a social process often with definable goals, it may have unanticipated biological and cultural effects upon those populations. What these are becomes an important point of departure for a full understanding of warfare for the human species. Specifically, does warfare lead to some kind of genetic selection? What possible effects does it have upon demography? What does it do to an ongoing cultural system? What short- and long-range psychological effects does it have upon populations experiencing it?

Frank Livingstone, a geneticist and physical anthropologist taking a long-term view, believes that warfare has little if any effect upon demographic and genetic variables:

> The last two World Wars have been responsible for enormous numbers of deaths, but it is nevertheless questionable as to whether they have had any permanent effect on the demography of the populations involved. Certainly the effects of war on the birth and death rates have caused a populational decrease. ("The Effects of Warfare on the Biology of the Human Species," p. 5)

> Given the negligible effects of modern warfare on the size of human populations, it would seem to follow that it has little effect on genetic evolution. As Haldane (1953) has emphasized, those forces which tend to limit the size of the population have the greatest effect as agents of natural selection. Aside from the effects of ionizing radiation on mutation, warfare would most likely influence the two other forces of evolution, natural selection and migration. . . . In this way warfare can account in part for the variability and distribution of genetic characteristics among human populations, but marked genetic differences, whether actual or postulated, must be due to natural selection. (p. 6)

Livingstone asserts that on the basis of population statistics modern warfare does not have much effect on the ongoing evolution of man. He counters the frequently stated contention of eugenists that modern warfare eliminates the weak by pointing out that only the most fit are selected for combat

and many of these are killed. Their chances of dying therefore go up. It is interesting to note in this respect that the reverse argument has also been used, namely, that only the
most fit survive war. With the ravages of civilian populations
this argument could be extended even to those who stay behind. But Livingstone sees little value in either type of explanation since, "first of all, however, the amount of possible
selection is small since the percentage of the population
killed in warfare itself is so minimal as to be ineffective." (p.
7)

In contrast to modern warfare, which deals with the en-
gagement of enormous populations, primitive warfare takes
place between small social units. Under these conditions
there would be a higher probability of selection and genetic
change if the kill frequency were high. Thus there is the possibility that warfare among early hunting peoples could have
had an effect on the evolution of modern man. Livingstone
cites data which suggests that the percentage of males killed
in tribal warfare is in fact considerably higher than in modern war. Death rates in such groups appear to run from 14 to
25%.

> I think the evidence from areas still inhabited by hunters or
> primitive agriculturalists who are not under the control of a
> national power indicates the same conclusion, and thus by im-
> plication that warfare has been a major agent of natural selec-
> tion. Warfare could also have been a major factor determining
> the dispersion of human populations at this cultural level, so
> that it would affect the other forces of evolution. The popula-
> tion size and consequently the amount of genetic drift, the
> amount of inbreeding, and the amount of gene flow among
> groups are all effected by population dispersion. (pp. 9–10)

Among those factors which might be effected by natural
selection through warfare Livingstone includes fighting abil-

ity and size and strength, but he indicates how tricky this
problem can be when he notes:

> Of course, in order to be a selective factor success in warfare
> has to be related to size and strength and not to ability to ride
> horses, shoot poison arrows, or sneak quietly through the jun-
> gle. In any case warfare may have been one contributing fac-
> tor to body size differences, but there were surely other selec-
> tive factors such as climate or nutrition. (pp. 10–11)

Livingstone turns finally to the psychological question
raised by Lorenz and Ardrey among other authors, namely,
the possible contribution of primitive warfare to such psychological factors as aggression. He responds as follows:

> Implicit in these suggestions is the assumption that innate ag-
> gression is the major explanation for human warfare. If this is
> accepted, then it implies further that differences in the
> amount of warfare among human populations is due to vary-
> ing amounts of this genetic trait. So we are back to the expla-
> nation that the plains Indians waged war because they were
> warlike. In the past this has not been a useful approach to the
> problem, but to reject this as an adequate explanation of
> human warfare does not mean that there are no genetic differ-
> ences in behavior which are due to selection by warfare. (p.
> 11)

What these differences are, or could be, is left open by Livingstone, and so they must be, since one can speculate just as
well about the evolution of group cohesion and cooperation
as that of aggressivity. And by now it should be quite clear
that, whatever relationships may exist between aggression
and war, they are certainly mediated by a wide range of intermediate variables more important than psychological determinants which themselves are determined by a combination of genetic and sociological variables. The best that can
be said for the aggression hypothesis is that aggression can be

mobilized in the service of warlike behavior under the proper circumstances. The best that can be said for the genetic hypothesis concerning aggression is that there may be genetic differences in aggression thresholds between individuals (some may be more excitable than others) and that it is at least conceivable that average thresholds may also vary from group to group. Even here, however, it must be reiterated that genetics is only part of the story concerning the threshold level at which some stimulus will induce behavior. Thresholds are part of behavior and they are subject to modification by environmental variables just like most other aspects of behavior. A discussion of war therefore demands that the aggression hypothesis be left far behind.

Livingstone's concern has been with the long-term effects of war on populations, but what of the short-term effects? And what of its effect on culture itself? The answer to these questions depends, of course, upon the type of war, the environmental background in which it is fought, and its duration. Long-term destructive wars beginning with the nation state have certainly taken their toll of both the military and civilian populations through direct destruction of the stream of normal life. Wars in Europe have contributed to vast epidemics, particularly of cholera, typhus, and the plague. These diseases occur when, for any reason, the normal course of life is severely disrupted. As far as the great plague epidemics of Europe are concerned there are two schools of thought with alternative views concerning the direction of causality. Some scholars have suggested that the plague caused widespread disruptions of the population, others have said that demographic conditions, along with economic deprivation led both to wars and to plague outbreaks. At the present time the latter view has more supporting evidence. (See Roberts, "The

Place of Plague in English History," 1967) Nonetheless, the relationship in the popular mind between war and epidemics is not farfetched. For destructive war has the effect of breaking down the established behavioral system, particularly public health and sanitation, as well as standards of nutrition. In addition the psychological stress to which a population is subjected may increase vulnerability to disease.

In a recent paper ("War and Disease," 1968), I suggested that the Vietnam war because of its long duration, the climate in which it is being fought, and the type of war it is, has created a situation in which disease becomes a major danger to the population at large. Disease rates (cf. WHO Report on Epidemiological situation in South Vietnam, 1968), particularly of infectious diseases such as plague, cholera, and malaria mounted steadily in South Vietnam with escalation in spite of attempts by local and international authorities to maintain public health services. The eventual toll on the population cannot even be estimated.

A tropical climate with its complex ecology is capable of supporting a wide variety of species, including parasites. When such an environment is densely populated the health balance of the inhabitants is in constant danger. Infectious disease, while never under complete control, is dampened by local hygiene practices and through Western-oriented public health and treatment procedures. Guerrilla warfare in which battle lines are disrupted can lead to a breakdown in both types of defense. Long-term disruptions of the ecological balance through massive bombing and use of napalm increase the possibility that disease will spread, since they create new relationships between vectors (mosquitoes, flies, etc.) and humans. The displacement of populations with forced and panic-induced voluntary migrations to the cities places strains on public health systems and sanitation even in those zones in which there has been no or only light destruction. Nutritional problems under these conditions are also likely to become severe. The movement of large segments of the population may expose individuals to disease organisms against which they have little immunity. Malaria parasites, for example, tend to produce an acquired immunity in local populations which may be lost when such individuals come into contact with genetic variants of parasites specific to other zones. Psychological factors may be important as well in lowering resistance to disease, and such an effect may persist well after the restoration of peace and a return to normal conditions. Thus Wolf ("Stressors as a Cause of Disease," 1960) has presented data which suggest that for as yet unknown reasons prisoners of war who have suffered psychological and physiological deprivation continue as high disease risks long after their return to civilian life. In addition, he found that many of the diseases occurring in this group could not be directly related to the specific physical conditions of the prison experience.

The destruction which accompanies war varies in extent with the methods of warfare employed, the environment in which war is waged, the duration of conflict, and the number and segments of the populations involved. From the point of view of culture, warfare may have an effect on the direction of culture change leading to the disruption and reorganization of a behavioral system, and even to innovations which in the long run produce adaptation. On the other hand, mobilization for war can lead to social regimentation which impedes change and which may outlive disturbed contitions. The role which warfare has played in maintaining or in changing behavioral systems has not been well studied by anthropologists and sociologists, but it would seem to me that such effects may far outweigh any genetic effects it might have.

In sum, warfare cannot be explained in genetic terms, nor is a hypothetical instinct for aggression adequate. War may have severe short-range consequences on a population affecting both health and the behavioral system. It does not appear to have long-range demographic or genetic effects, although in the early stages of human evolution it may have played a role in selection. What this role may have been, however, is by no means clear and the acceptance of the aggression hypothesis is based on an oversimplified concept of the evolutionary process as well as on the unproven assumption that early man was constantly at war with his neighbors. The functions which war may serve to maintain or change cultural systems are manifold, but in each case they must be demonstrated with hard data. Few such data exist in the anthropological literature. Whatever these functions may be, it is important to note that they cannot be used as an explanation for the *causes* of war, for once introduced into a system a particular behavioral feature may have consequences for that system which are unrelated to its origin. Furthermore, can one assume that, because war functions to maintain some system, it is the only means by which such a system can be maintained?

# BIOLOGY AND THE SOCIAL SCIENCES: THE HUMAN IMPERATIVE

MUCH OF ANTHROPOLOGY developed as a reaction to an over-emphasis placed on biology in the analysis of human behavior. Anthropologists have quite successfully demonstrated that cultural and not biological factors are responsible for behavioral differences found among the world's populations. They have also demonstrated that culture is the major determinant in human existence and that while the capacity for acquiring culture is *largely* a biological phenomenon (early social experience is also crucial for cultural acquisition) its expression depends upon learning. In the rush to reform our view of man early anthropology neglected to investigate the biological basis of this capacity, but such a lacuna has been remedied in recent years by attention to behavioral as well as physical evolution.

The details of this behavioral evolution and its morphological-physiological correlates have yet to be filled in. The study of the fossil and archeological record along with the analysis of similarities and differences between subhuman primate behavior and human behavior provides further clues to this evolution. What must not be lost sight of is the important fact that, while such data provide a basis for the understanding of the human species as a species, they cannot go very far in explaining behavioral differences among human groups. This is why Morris' *The Naked Ape* is successful only as a prolegomena to the study of man and why it is a dismal failure when it comes to the essentials of human history.

Nevertheless, I believe that a materialistic biological framework is necessary for an understanding of human behavior. We must not lose sight of the fact that man is subject to the same selective forces which nature has impressed upon other species, and that his means of dealing with environmental problems involves biological solutions which include a subtle interplay between culture (which is itself the result of biological evolution) and genetics. Culture is not only a product of biology, it is man's continuing adaptive device in the process of accommodation to the environment.

Some anthropologists have claimed that since man is capable of creating his own environment through culture he is free of biological restraints. It is true that technological mastery, particularly since the industrial revolution, has done much to modify the environmental setting. Nonetheless, each modification creates new selective pressures which continue to operate on both genetic and cultural levels. René Dubos, a microbiologist with a strong interest in historical epidemiology, has illustrated this point very well in his books *Man Adapting* and *The Mirage of Health*. He has shown that public health problems change with environmental modifications but they do not disappear. This is true also of the means employed in the exploitation of natural resources which involve both their destruction and their distribution, as well as environmental pollution.

Genes are responsible for man's capacity to acquire culture. They are also responsible for the basis of other capacities, the potential for a wide range of behaviors. The expression of these traits depends upon the environment in which maturation takes place. Different human populations may have somewhat different potentials, particularly small isolated populations living in extreme environmental conditions, but it must be borne in mind that while genes may provide different probabilities for behavior they do not produce the actual behavior itself. Thus different environmental conditions (including education) can produce the same behavioral results on different genetic backgrounds. Individuals with very similar genetic backgrounds can be very different. We must not forget that anthropology has already demonstrated that major (even minor) behavioral differences between human groups depend upon culture.

This does not exclude the possibility that culturally based behavior affects genetic structure and that alterations in genetic patterns may facilitate cultural adaptation to specific environments. Protection against a disease, for example, can allow a culture to expand into an environment which might otherwise be hostile to survival. In addition, man can perfectly well overcome certain genetic disabilities through culture. If more and more humans come to wear glasses as the result of "bad eye genes" the success of the human species will not be threatened. Eyeglasses are a legitimate substitute for better eyes. Nonetheless, any cultural trait which raises the fertility level of individuals who otherwise would be at a genetic disadvantage is going to alter the frequency of that gene in the population.

In human evolution the genetic process has given birth to a new and more efficient form of code system which is capable of rapid change and which can be transferred from organism to organism through learning and is thus freed of slower somatic pathways. This new code system, culture, is as responsive to selective forces as the old one, DNA, and interacts with it to some extent.

Human behavior in specific groups is based largely on a shared cognitive system. This cognitive system consists of classifications in which the environmental field (including other human beings) is divided according to an arbitrary but traditional system. Out of this classification system develops a set of rules for action (action which varies from forms of etiquette to methods of production). When these rules are put into play, selection begins. It is only when ideas are acted out in real behavior that they enter into the dialectical process between the organism or system and the environment. Once selection has begun it will itself influence further choices in overt behavior and in the formation of new classifications. For instance, we are now discovering the dangerous effects of the automobile on our environment and our health. This will lead to new adjustments and attitudes ranging from technological change to legal change. The relationship between the cognitive system and overt behavior is never direct or perfect because 1) the system is always changing in response to environmental pressures and changes which originate in the behavior of individuals, 2) the cognitive system may serve as a blind; that is, rules may be vague specifically to allow for a certain amount of flexibility in behavior (The United States Constitution is a perfect example of this), and 3) the rule system may serve as a justification for behavior which has developed independently in the selection process. The reasons people give for doing something may in fact be nothing more than a rationalization for their behavior, (a means of keeping the cognitive system consistent). These are the well-known explanations after the fact.

As a Darwinian social scientist, I am more interested in the effects of behavior on the environment and vice versa than I am in the content of the cognitive system. I want to know how actual behavior (which is easier to study than some internalized abstract system) affects actual events and is affected by them. Differences between this or that cognitive system may obscure real similarities in the adaptive process. I do not mean to say that cognitive systems have no effect on the direction and rate of change, however. The organization of thought, particularly in the form of theories about the environment, certainly does shape the range of choices that can be made in response to a given situation. But once action is taken, feedback from the environment will act to shape further behavior. The process is the same in genetic change and in cultural change. New elements (mutations, innovations, borrowed items) either fit the existing system or they do not, they either add to the efficiency of the system *vis à vis* the environment or they do not. In genetic evolution we can say that the environment rewards or punishes the population depending upon the effect of that particular gene in that particular environment. Although mutations are random accidental events, they can be seen as environment testing devices. They represent a probing of the environment which when successful produces a gain for the species. Culture involves very much the same type of process. The environment is tested through behavior and responds selectively; that is, the result of behavior in a specific setting produces either loss or gain (medicines either work or they do not, planting techniques either work or they do not). It may also be neutral. Another way of looking at this process is to draw an analogy with the learning theory of B. F. Skinner. In his theory known as operant conditioning an experimenter manipulates the environment in response to random behavior on the part of an organism. When an organism behaves in a way approaching some planned modification it is rewarded immediately. This reward reinforces the modification of behavior. Each more nearly perfect response is rewarded and the desired behavior is therefore shaped. This is similar to the process which occurs in genetic change and selection. Mutations are random, but once an adaptive trend is established it tends to continue just as long as the possibilities inherent in the variation are not exhausted. Good moves on the part of the species (successful mutations) are rewarded. Thus the development of the hand in primates has been shaped by selecting from a range of mutations, those which favored the development of an opposable thumb (opposed to the other fingers), and a prehensile (grasping) hand. The development of nails in place of claws, and the development of good eye-hand coordination allowed the refined hand-tool to be used effectively in carrying and the manipulation of tools.

Evolution has favored a trend in the direction of increased capacity for learning and flexible behavior. This trend began early in phylogeny and occurs concurrently with more stereotyped behavior which depends more directly upon genetic patterning. The development of learning and so-called innate behavior cannot be separated into two distinct compartments. In many species, and in many types of behavior, there is a subtle interaction between the two. Increased learning capacity, accompanied by an increased ability to respond to the environment, provides important selective advantages. An organism located in a changing environment can change its behavior through learning in direct response to environmental pressures, while changes in behavior which depend upon mutation can only help succeeding generations.

The evolution of culture and language allows for the development of a tradition within the species (similar to the tradition built into the genetic code) but also for change based upon some sense of direction (planning ahead). Just as the genetic code has grown and become more complex in terms of the amount of information which it carries, the cultural code has also grown. Certain ideas and techniques are impossible without certain forerunners in culture. Technological sequences have been known for some time. The simplest and most obvious of these is the change from hunting and gathering to agriculture. The city and urban civilization occurred relatively late in human history because it was dependent upon preceding forms of technology, as well as upon new types of social organization.

The gathering of information concerning sequences tells us little about the essential processes of evolution which involve the sources of change and the process of natural selection. Some anthropologists, the first of whom was V. Gordon Childe, have attempted to sort out the environmental elements which favor the development of large population conglomerates and eventually urban civilization. Childe pointed out long ago that, once these new forms of social and technological organization had developed in the context of a specific environment, they could spread to less favorable areas. Thus for Childe it was no accident that civilization developed in river valleys which were hemmed in by desert areas. In such environments agriculture could be intense (due to restoration of fertility through seasonal flooding) but would also be limited in space so that growing populations would be confined geographically. He also saw an uneven distribution of resources among a series of such riverine populations as a stimulus for trade, which in turn led to the development of full-time specialists who depended upon others for subsistence. These same traders eventually developed a tally system to keep track of their growing economic activities. Later on, writing developed out of these tally systems.

This is essentially a cultural materialist interpretation of the rise of civilization, for the economic organization including technology and the organization of work are taken as the major impetus for change. Recently Robert Adams of the University of Chicago has attempted to show how the development of ideology itself led to significant changes in the development of the great Middle Eastern civilizations. His argument is similar to one used by Max Weber, the German sociologist, against Marx in reference to the origin of capitalism. Weber saw the impetus for capitalism arising out of the Protestant Reformation in which man's attitude toward God and religion eventually led to the capitalist ethic which stimulated rational economic methods, the accumulation of capital, and its constant reinvestment in the system. Weber's own historical interpretation has not gone unchallenged and the reader who finds himself interested in this controversy should consult both Weber's *Protestant Ethic and the Rise of Capitalism* and R. H. Tawney's *Religion and the Rise of Capitalism*.

Biologists tell us much about all animals and therefore much about man, particularly his development as a species. But it is the students of human behavior specifically who, in the end, will lead us to a full understanding of ourselves. Comparative studies of different species will prove successful only when they highlight essential differences as well as essential similarities. Anthropologists, for their part, must not impede the dialogue by decrying ethology in general. The study of "human nature," limited, for example, as it is by the structuralist school of anthropology to speculation about the functioning of the human mind, will never give us much insight into the actual historical process of change and economic development. The instinct school will never be able to explain war or property or human territoriality on the basis of a few simple-minded analogies between birds and fish on one hand and what they think are essentially genetic processes in man on the other.

Let me return to the genetic model for a moment and reconstruct out of it what I think are the essential elements which yield the human experience, underlining again that this model accounts only for our beginnings and our capacities, our probabilities and our limitations. It can never account for the specifics or even the full range of possibilities of human behavior.

While I think it makes better sense to look at close phylogenetic relatives in the search for our own biological foundations, I shall begin with one trait which all animals have in common and which also persists in man: irritability. This involves the sensing and response of animals to stimuli such as light, temperature, or gravity. Now I must admit at once that this is even more vague and general than the concept of aggression, but I think it is also more useful. Irritability produces a basic adaptation which becomes elaborated according to the environmental problems faced by an organism and its own level of phylogenetic development. It depends upon the elaboration of the nervous system and includes systems of reception and response. In order to respond to some change in the environmental field an organism must sense that change. Perceptive capacities tend to become highly refined with the development of complex nervous systems but many lower organisms are quite capable of responding to minute changes in certain environmental variables, those which are crucial for their survival. Leeches, for example, can perceive minute amounts of blood in solution and certain biting insects, including mosquitoes, are sensitive to the $CO_2$ exuded by their prey. Among mammals the five senses are quite well developed, but certain of them take precedence in accordance with the behavioral requirements of the species. Ruminants (animals which eat grasses) generally have a good sense of smell and of hearing, which allows them to escape from potential predators. Primates, originally adapted to life in the trees, have a diminished sense of smell, but a marked superiority over ground dwellers in vision. Primates are the only mammals to possess stereoscopic color vision which allows them to perceive depth (obviously advantageous when jumping from branch to branch) and color. In addition to this, primates have developed good eye-hand coordination which allows them to take well coordinated action in response to environmental signals.

The connection between perceptive mechanisms and essential action or behavior is widespread. An organism must be able to use the information gathered by its perceptive mechanisms. Responses vary, depending on the phylogenetic capacities and the particular type of stimulus. Very simple organisms may merely be capable of increasing random motion in the presence of some stimulus. Such activity, known as *kinesis,* successfully removes the organism from obnoxious stimuli, since it comes to rest only when it has escaped the field of excitation. Kinesis, however, is not very economical. *Taxis,* a slightly more complicated form of response, allows an organism to react directly and therefore more efficiently moving toward positive stimuli and away from specific irritants. Taxis provides the beginning of positive as well as negative behavior. Organisms not only improve their environmental field through escape from obnoxious stimuli, but can move into a more favorable zone.

Beyond the level of simple kinesis and taxis, behavior becomes extremely complicated. Organisms may respond to cues emitted by other organisms of the same or different species, thus participating in a form of communication and/or they may respond to environmental cues with highly complex behavioral responses that lead to a marked restructuring of the environment. Web spinning in spiders and nest building in birds are examples of this. Organisms may respond to threats by retreating out of the dangerous field or they may defend themselves. They may also attack members of another species if they are predators, or members of their own species under a set of rather specific releasers (cues which release behavior). The latter behavior is what we call aggression. Aggression may be an adaptive response to disturbances in the environmental field. It is evident that in man there are no specific releasers and that the aggressive response, when it occurs, is far from stereotypic.

As I have already noted, the ability of an organism to respond to a stimulus depends first upon its ability to perceive it. Stimulus thresholds vary by species, and also by organism.

They can also vary in relation to degree, frequency, and type of experience. Interestingly, the experience does not necessarily have to involve the specific releaser. The kind of relationship a mammal or a bird has with its mother or siblings may affect its perceptive abilities and activities at a later stage. There appears to be a widespread relationship between stimulation in general, in early stages of development, and the ability of an animal to respond later to specific sets of cues. The relationship between development and later activity is not well understood but it can be safely said that the more researchers concentrate on infant experience the more they discover how crucial it is to behavioral output at later stages.

Let me narrow the focus to mammals alone. Mammals are warm-blooded. This allows them to live in a wide range of environments closed to species unable to regulate body temperature. Mammals must, however, maintain a high activity level (let us omit hibernation) in order to feed a rapid metabolic system. Not only are mammals viviparous (bearing live young), but the female of the species nurtures her young. As a byproduct of nurturance, a psychological relationship develops between mother and offspring. Mothering is known to have behavioral effects on every species thus far tested in the laboratory. Mammals also display an increased development of the. cerebral cortex relative to other animals, which allows a high order of perceptual discrimination, memory storage, and the association of various types of data. This development, as well as a long dependency of the offspring on adult animals, particularly the mother, and in some cases other females as well, is most highly developed in primates, particularly man. Increased learning ability and dependency create favorable conditions for the extensive modification of behavioral traits including those which are based on genetic transmission. Such learning also allows the stripping away of much genetically programmed behavior. This constitutes an evolutionary gain because reactions can be adjusted in appropriate ways to a wide and changing array of environmental stimuli. With the advent of man the learning of a tradition (culture) maintains behavioral continuity, but at the same time provides a relatively high degree of behavioral flexibility. The less innate human behavior is, the more adaptive is it likely to be, since man behaves in variable social and environmental contexts.

Learning is facilitated not only by the social experience in which at early stages the offspring is protected by parent organisms, but also by another behavioral feature which I think is found in all mammalian species, that is, play. Play involves an unusually safe exploratory manipulation of the environment. Play fighting, for example, does not lead to death or injury, and playful attempts at nurturance behavior which fail do not lead to starvation of the young since the mother does the actual feeding. Omar Moore has pointed out that play in humans involves an active testing of the environment. It is thus a learning situation in which reward reinforces successful behavior and in which there is little danger of punishment. Play is a form of instrumental conditioning similar to the kind described by Skinnerian psychology.

Another widespread mammalian trait, found to be particularly strong in primates and man, is identification, the social bonding of an organism to another or a group of organisms, usually of the same species. Identification is a product of the social process. While the ability to identify may be genetically determined, the degree and type of identification depends solely on the social experience of the animal. In the case of man, if some identification with a social group does not occur, an individual will have difficulty surviving. This is because man *qua* man must be social. An individual human cannot behave in what we take to be a human way without identifying himself with some social group and then acting out this identification in a socially defined meaningful way. Individuals who have been deprived of a normal socialization experience have problems in both self identity (which is actually defined in terms of social identification with others) and group identity. In severe cases of isolation in childhood individuals become permanently impaired: they may be physiologically human but behaviorally are not quite so. While identification is a product of the social process, it is also a by-product of biological structure. Human infants cannot survive alone for very long without nurturance. The nurturance period is also the time at which the central nervous system matures. Lasting patterns of social behavior including perceptive capacities are developed during this stage. The biological prerequisites for human survival create the conditions for a certain type of social development which is determined by tradition and a normal range of individual variations in the socialization process. Thus the development of humans is social-psychological rather than strictly genetic although it is subject to genetic limitations.

Identification is thus very open ended. It can be associated with a territory (which is itself socially defined) but it need not be. Individuals can and do identify with sets of individuals, with social groups, and with sets of ideas as well. Also individual human beings are capable of identifying with more than one set or type of phenomena. For man, at least, identification is more real and fundamental than territoriality, which is only one possible outcome of the identification process.

Aggression, which is one possible response to stimulation, may be, but is not necessarily, tied to territorial or other identification. Frequently aggression is expressed within a particular defined social segment (siblings or co-wives, married couples, kin groups, etc.) and appears to be the result of conflicts which result in part from the rule system which imposes limits upon the behavior of members. As I have already pointed out, aggression is released by a set of culturally and sometimes idiosyncratically determined cues. The objects which aggressive action may be turned against (including people) are also defined culturally. Individuals may break these rules, but they may face sanctions for doing so. There is evidence that frustration frequently leads to aggression, but this is not to say it is the only releaser. Individuals can be conditioned to respond aggressively to a set of cues even when frustration is not present (although it may have been present at the time of conditioning).

Aggression can be diverted onto substitute objects. In this way what are essentially individual psychological problems can be turned through cultural mechanisms to organized hostility of one group toward another. It is here and *only* here that warfare and aggression are linked, for, in general, the problem of aggression is psychological while the problem of war is social. Aggressive action involves individual conditioning including direct aggression training which can be and has been observed and quantified in many cultures. It also includes other aspects of the socialization process which affect threshold levels, identity, and the ability of an individual to engage in group processes.

War involves group structure, group identity, and group ethos, and can be undertaken without prior "aggressive" commitment. Some soldiers undoubtedly kill aggressively, others defensively, while still others do what they are told to do out of fear that to do otherwise would lead to severe sanctions. The planning of war is a different matter. The fact that we label one side as an aggressor should not allow us to fall into a semantic trap. It is necessarily true that one side in war is the instigator of action, but, as we have seen in the Iroquois case, wars are fought for ends which are often unrelated to aggressive "feelings." Wars result from the interaction of populations in relation to environmental variables. Sometimes they are fought for territory, sometimes for women, sometimes for revenge, sometimes for ritual reasons, and, as is frequent in the case of modern warfare, for politico-economic reasons.

It is imperative that the concept of aggression be separated in the minds of laymen and professionals from ideas about war. This is a blinder allowing for the continued exploitation of some human groups by others. It hides the vast wastage of resources and human life which is accelerating at an increasing rate in present history.

It has been suggested that play can be substitued for war through the institutionalization of aggressive games. Such a solution is even offered by Lorenz at the end of *On Aggression*. This solution is likely to be unsuccessful. Games may, in fact, be used as an institutionalized means of preparing men for war. There is no evidence that game playing lowers aggression. In fact, there is contrary evidence. Participants and spectators of violent sports may feel a surge of aggression in themselves as a result of direct stimulation. Games may serve to bring together people who are mistrustful and who know little of one another, but the effect on war of such play will be determined by the war makers, not the organizers of the games themselves. The belief that one can offer psychological cures for social problems is a delusion; perhaps it even diverts attention from the real causes of war.

It is imperative to face the fact that war cannot be reduced to some simple set of biological principles. If aggression is a human problem, and I agree that it is, it must be solved through a better understanding of those processes which transform man the animal into man the social being. The social sciences, particularly psychology, anthropology, and sociology, have already provided us with an understanding of those processes which are involved in the formation of individual personalities, and social groups. They have also made it quite clear that the simple biological explanations offered by Lorenz and Ardrey are meaningless.

Aggression theories teach us that man is by nature self-destructive. A full look at the evidence shows that by nature man is neither good nor bad. The romantic fallacy is wrong, but no more wrong than the concept of original sin. The evidence tells us that man is not driven by instincts but rather that he is born with a set of capacities, potentials which are developed or thwarted and given direction by early learning and the cultural process. Among these is the potential for exploration which can manifest itself in man as creativity. This is coupled with an apparent need for stimulation and an identification with socially defined objects, either humans, ideals, territory, or any combination of these. The future of man depends upon the way in which these capacities are expressed and developed. Man has another quality perhaps in part also biological; the tendency to avoid ambiguity. Erich Fromm has written about this in *Escape from Freedom*. Culture as a system provides individuals with a set of devices which allow one human to predict the social behavior of another in a given set of social circumstances. Culture acts to restrain human action. Freud was the first to describe this process in *Civilization and Its Discontents*. He couched his argument in terms of conflict between warring instincts: those associated with life and creativity and those associated with aggression and death. I think that today these can be taken as allegorical. The true conflict is between necessary restraint (the need for a system) and man's ability to break the bounds of his self-constructed system. Social systems cannot run without rules, but the rigid imposition of these rules is destructive.

Sewell Wright, a mathematical geneticist, has told us that evolution is speeded up when a species is divided into small semi-isolated populations which share genetic material only sporadically. Separation leads to diversity among groups, particularly when in small populations accidental variation can become fixed rapidly into the gene pool. The occasional recombination of genetic material provides natural selection with the raw material out of which new trends may be established. Crossing between related, but different, groups increases the opportunities for rapid selection. I think the same thing is true for culture. Man has advanced technologically and socially as often through the process of borrowing as through the process of innovation within culture. It is my hope, therefore, that cultural differences will continue to exist in a world which is still rich in variety. There are also good humanistic reasons for preserving differences. Each time a language disappears, each time a tradition falls victim to mass culture and machine technology, our poverty increases. This is not to say that I wish to keep primitive man primitive. I have already indicated that the process of borrowing is necessary for continuing evolution. But to be really free the borrowing must not be attached to an oppressive ideology. Individuals must choose in relation to their own system and needs, not on the basis of what we in the West think will be good for them. Too often this amounts to what we really think will be good for us. The real tragedy of the modern world comes when solutions are imposed by vested interests. Freedom of choice is too often an empty slogan, and change more often than not leads to a kind of dehumanization. The African youth is not free as Ardrey suggests to go to the city for excitement and pleasure. He goes because he is driven by economic necessity imposed from the outside. His longing is to return home with his youth intact. Instead he is freed of economic bondage only when he is no longer of use to the system, a system which has forced him into economic dependence and has given him in return nothing of lasting value.

We all know that nations are no longer isolated from one another. In Darwinian terms the entire world has become man's single environment. The survival of our species depends upon a global adjustment. It is the human imperative that such an adjustment include peace and equity. Neither will be achieved in spite of our capacity for rapid technological innovation unless such innovation is carefully examined in terms of its potential environmental effect and applied to the problem of more equal rather than less equal distribution. Local problems will have to be examined within local contexts. The obvious may turn out to be false. For example recent advances in productivity and medicine appear to have caused an unprecedented rate of growth of the world's population. Before we innocently accept the dictum that population growth occurs automatically as soon as modern medicine appears upon the scene, however, we must account for such differences in demographic increase as have occurred, for example, in Java on one hand and Sumatra on the other. While Sumatra's population remained relatively stable, Java's population increased from about 5 million to about 70 million in seventy years. The Javanese population explosion can best be explained as an adaptation to economic needs under a system of agriculture (wet rice cultivation) which requires constant labor intensification with little or no increase in land or capital input. Such a system of plantation agriculture was imposed on Indonesia by the Dutch during their colonial rule (Ben White in a personal communication).

The poor health, poor nutrition, and population shifts which are frequently documented among the world's peasants may not be due, as has often been supposed, to their superstitious natures or ideological rigidity. A system may be adjusted within strictly imposed limits, and maladaptation may result from a loss of ability to control resources. Conditions imposed by some exploiting power, extranational or a segment of a national conglomeration, may be the major cause of adaptive breakdown. Population density and fertility strategies may be the result of labor needs and particular patterns of internal and external exploitation. The pattern of monocropping (planting only a single crop which is marketed) so often found among peasants is an imposed response to an economic system over which local populations have little or no control. Monocropping reduces or eliminates local garden plots as more and more land is put into production and may thus contribute to caloric deficiency or other forms of malnutrition. It may also produce irreversible environmental degradation.

Whatever the cause or causes, the world *is* undergoing a rapid increase in population. This demographic change has implications in relation not only to food production and distribution but to the very nature of social structure itself, including the organization of megapopulations even in technologically advanced countries. We know very little at present

about the effects of overcrowding on the physiological, morphological, and psychological systems of the human being.
We do not even know what crowding really means in cultural terms, since man appears able to constantly redefine his
social environment. What may be stressful to old-timers may
be reinterpreted by a younger generation as neutral or even
positively stimulating. Stress of all types is a physiological
problem, but stress tolerance probably varies along two di-
mensions, cultural and biological. Individual and group differences in stress tolerance are probably due to both biological factors and cultural experience.

For a long time philosophers, some anthropologists, and
certainly many laymen saw a great distinction between primitive man and ourselves. Our solutions to problems were rational, the primitive's solutions were riddled with mysticism
and superstition. Anthropological data show clearly, however,
that non-western cultures, primitive and otherwise, are ori-
ented toward problem-solving in the same manner as our
own. While the solutions may not be as efficient, technologically speaking, as ours, they often represent rather fine-grain
adaptations to difficult environmental circumstances. In fact,
government organizations specifically involved in aid projects
in the "third world" sometimes find that their programs make
less sense than the "natives" own behavioral adaptation. This
is not to say that there are no imbalances in the world and no
economic or social problems, but we often overlook the possibility that these may be of recent vintage and the result of
present or former colonization.

The "American" solution to socio-economic problems often
involves greater energy extraction than is necessary or desir-
able. We are radical in relation to environmental exploitation
and generally conservative in our relations with established

power structures. This results in a greater separation of rich and poor which is translated as progress, as witnessed by rates of growth or industrialization. As Myrdal has said:

> Often it even happened that new privileges and new privileged groups were created by the colonial power in order to stabilize its rule over a colony.
>
> There is no doubt that a similar mechanism has been operating after the liquidation of colonialism and that, now as before, it also has its counterpart in relation to those underdeveloped countries that were politically independent, primarily in Latin America. This is the main justification for the use of the term "neocolonialism". (Gunnar Myrdal, *The Challenge of World Poverty*, p. 85)

These policies are justified in terms of political and economic expediency, for it is said that growth can occur only under a stable system and that growth itself acts as a deterrent to communism. Meanwhile, the struggles which emerge within and between nations are reduced by such authors as Ardrey, and to a lesser extent Lorenz, to the simple expression of aggression and territoriality. These authors and other members of their camp have become the vanguard of the *status quo*. Their blatant biological determinism only serves to blunt our awareness of the complexities of human existence. Peace and equity can be attained only when man's creative capacities are developed and put to work unselfishly for the benefit of the entire species. The biological foundation exists. The cultural possibilities are infinite. Whether or not man will come to terms with himself and his environment remains to be seen.

# BIBLIOGRAPHY

This bibliography contains works cited in the text and suggested readings. Works are grouped by subject.

## EVOLUTION AND GENETICS

Darwin, Charles. *The Origin of Species by Means of Natural Selection*. London, John Murray, 1859.

Dobzhansky, Thodosius. *Genetics of The Evolutionary Process*. New York, Columbia University Press, 1970.

Gajdusek, Carlton. "Factors Governing the Genetics of Primitive Human Populations," *Cold Spring Harbor Symposium on Quantitative Biology*, XXIX (1944): 121–36.

Glass, David C., ed. *Neurophysiology and Emotion*. New York, Rockefeller University Press, 1967.

Glass, David C., ed. *Environmental Influences.* New York, Rockefeller University Press, 1968.

Hirsch, Jerry, ed. *Behavior Genetic Analysis.* New York, McGraw Hill, 1967.

Huxley, Julian. *Evolution The Modern Synthesis.* New York, Harper and Brothers, 1943.

Keith, Sir Arthur. *Essays on Human Evolution.* London, Watts, 1946.

Lasker, Gabriel W., ed. *The Processes of Ongoing Human Evolution.* Detroit, Wayne State University Press, 1960.

Livingstone, Frank. "The Effects of Warfare on The Biology of the Human Species," in *War: The Anthropology of Armed Conflict and Aggression,* edited by Morton Fried, *et al.* (New York, Natural History Press, 1968), pp. 3–15.

Mayr, Ernst. *Animal Species and Evolution.* Cambridge, The Belknap Press of Harvard University Press, 1963.

Roe, Anne, and George Gaylord Simpson. *Behavior and Evolution.* New Haven, Yale University Press, 1958.

Scott, John Paul, and John L. Fuller. *Genetics and The Social Behavior of The Dog.* University of Chicago Press, 1965.

Simpson, George Gaylord. *The Major Features of Evolution.* New York, Columbia University Press, 1953.

Tax, Sol, ed. *The Evolution of Life.* University of Chicago Press, 1960.

——, ed. *The Evolution of Man.* University of Chicago Press, 1960.

——, and Charles Callender, ed. *Issues in Evolution.* University of Chicago Press, 1960.

Washburn, Sherwood L., ed. *Social Life of Early Man.* Chicago, Aldine Publishing Co., 1961.

Wright, Sewall. "The Foundations of Population Genetics," in *Heritage From Mendel,* edited by Alexander Brink. Madison, University of Wisconsin Press, 1967.

ETHOLOGY AND PRIMATE BEHAVIOR,
INCLUDING CRITICAL STUDIES

Altmann, Stuart A., ed. *Social Communication among Primates.* University of Chicago Press, 1967.

Ardrey, Robert. *African Genesis.* New York, Dell Publishing Co., 1961.

——. *The Territorial Imperative.* New York, Dell Publishing Co., 1966.

——. *The Social Contract.* New York, Atheneum, 1970.

Beatty, John. "Taking Issue With Lorenz on The Ute" in *Man and Aggression,* edited by Ashley Montagu, (New York, Oxford University Press, 1968), pp. 111–15.

Bigelow, Robert. *The Dawn Warriors: Man's Evolution Towards Peace.* Boston, Little, Brown and Co., 1969.

Carpenter, C. R. *Naturalistic Behavior of Non-human Primates.* University Park, Pa., Penn State University Press, 1964.

Darlington, C. D. *The Evolution of Man and Society.* New York, Simon & Schuster, 1969.

Dart, Raymond A. (1953) "The Predatory Transition From Ape To Man," *International Anthropological and Linguistic Review,* I (no. 4, 1953).

DeVore, Irven, ed. *Primate Behavior.* New York, Holt, Rinehart & Winston, 1965.

Etkin, William, ed. *Social Behavior and Organization among Vertebrates.* University of Chicago Press, 1964.

Harlow, Harry. "The Heterosexual Affectional System in Monkeys," *American Psychologist,* XVII (1962), 1–9.

Jay, Phyllis C., ed. *Primates: Studies in Adaptation and Variability.* New York, Holt, Rinehart & Winston, 1968.

Jolly, Allison. *Lemur Behavior.* University of Chicago Press, 1966.

Lorenz, Konrad. *On Aggression.* New York, Harcourt Brace,

1966; New York, Bantam Books, 1967. Page references are to Bantam Books edition.

———. *Studies in Animal and Human Behavior,* Vol. I. Cambridge, Harvard University Press, 1970.

Marler, Peter R., and William J. Hamilton, III, eds. *Mechanisms of Animal Behavior.* New York, John Wiley and Sons, Inc., 1966.

Morris, Desmond. *The Naked Ape.* New York, McGraw-Hill, 1967.

Schaller, George B. *The Mountain Gorilla.* University of Chicago Press, 1963.

Schiller, Claire H., ed. *Instinctive Behavior: The Development of a Modern Concept.* New York, International Universities Press, 1957.

Stewart, Omar C. "Lorenz/Margolin on the Ute," in *Man and Aggression,* edited by Ashley Montagu (New York, Oxford University Press, 1968), pp. 103–10.

Tiger, Lionel. *Men in Groups.* New York, Random House, 1969.

Washburn, Sherwood L. "Tools and Human Evolution," in *Human Variation and Origins,* edited by W. S. Laughlin and R. H. Osborne (San Francisco, W. H. Freeman & Co., 1967), pp. 169–82. Originally published 1960.

———, and Irven DeVore. "Social Life of Baboons," *Scientific American,* CCIV (no. 6, June, 1961), 61–71.

CULTURE, CULTURAL EVOLUTION,
AND HUMAN ECOLOGY

Adams, Robert McC. *The Rise of Urban Society.* Chicago, Aldine Publishing Co., 1965.

Alland, Alexander, Jr. *Evolution and Human Behavior.* New York, Natural History Press, 1967.

———. (1968) "War and Disease: An Anthropological

Perspective," in *War: The Anthropology of Armed Conflict and Aggression,* edited by Morton Fried, *et al.* (New York, Natural History Press, 1968), pp. 65–75.

Chagnon, Napoleon A. *Yanomamo: The Fierce People.* New York, Holt, Rinehart and Winston, 1968.

Childe, V. Gordon. *Man Makes Himself.* London, C. A. Watts & Co., 1936.

——. *Social Evolution.* New York, Henry Schuman, 1951.

Dentan, Robert K. *The Semai: A Nonviolent People of Malaya.* New York, Holt, Rinehart, and Winston, 1968.

Fried, Morton. *The Evolution of Political Society.* New York, Random House, 1968.

Geertz, Clifford. *Agricultural Involution.* Berkeley, University of California Press, 1963.

Harris, Marvin. *The Rise of Anthropological Theory.* New York, Thomas Crowell, 1968.

Howell, F. Clark, and Francois Bourliere, eds. *African Ecology and Evolution.* Chicago, Aldine Publishing Co., 1963.

Hunt, George T. *The Wars of the Iroquois.* Madison, University of Wisconsin Press, 1940.

Kluckhohn, Clyde. *Navajo Witchcraft.* Cambridge, Harvard University Press, 1944.

Leachman, J. Douglas. *Native Tribes of Canada.* Scarborough, Ontario, W. J. Gage Ltd., 1956.

Lee, Richard B., and Irven DeVore. *Man The Hunter.* Chicago, Aldine Publishing Co., 1968.

Mead, Margaret. *Continuities in Cultural Evolution.* New Haven, Yale University Press, 1964.

Myrdal, Gunnar. *The Challenge of World Poverty.* London, Penguin Books, 1971.

Roberts, R. S. "The Place of Plague in English History," *Royal Society of Medicine Proceedings,* LIX (1966), 101–5.

Sahlins, Marshall D. "La Première Société d'abondance," *Les Temps Moderne,* XXIV (1968), 641–80.

Sahlins, Marshall D., and Elman R. Service. *Evolution and Culture*. Ann Arbor, University of Michigan Press, 1960.

Sanders, William T., and Barbara Price. *Mesoamerica: The Evolution of a Civilization*. New York, Random House, 1968.

Service, Elman R. *Primitive Social Organization: An Evolutionary Perspective*. New York, Random House, 1962.

——. (1968) "War and Our Contemporary Ancestors," in *War: The Anthropology of Armed Conflict and Aggression*, edited by Morton Fried, *et al.* (New York, Natural History Press, 1968), pp. 160–69.

Spuhler, James, N., ed. *The Evolution of Man's Capacity for Culture*. Detroit, Wayne State University Press, 1959.

Steward, Julian H. (1955) *Theory of Culture Change*. Urbana, University of Illinois Press, 1955.

Turnbull, Colin. *The Forest People*. New York, Simon & Schuster, 1961.

Vayda, Andrew P. (1968) "Hypotheses About Functions of War," in *War: The Anthropology of Armed Conflict and Aggression*, edited by Morton Fried, *et al.* (New York, Natural History Press, 1968), pp. 85–91.

——. *Environment and Cultural Behavior*. New York, Natural History Press, 1969.

Weisenfeld, S. L. (1967) "Sickle Cell Trait in Human Biological and Cultural Evolution," *Science* (1967), CLVII, 1134–40.

White, Leslie. *The Evolution of Culture*. New York, McGraw-Hill, 1959.

Wolf, Harold G. "Stressors as a Cause of Disease," in *Stress and Psychiatric Disorders: The Proceedings of the Mental Health Research Fund 2nd Conference*, edited by J. M. Tanner (Oxford, Blackwells, 1960), pp. 17–31.

## MAN THE CREATIVE ANIMAL

Boas, Franz. *Race, Language and Culture.* New York, Mac-Millan Free Press Paperback edition, 1966. (Originally published, 1940.)

Dubos, René. *Mirage of Health.* New York, Doubleday (Anchor Books), 1961.

———. *Man Adapting.* New Haven, Yale University Press, 1965.

Fromm, Erich. *Escape from Freedom.* New York, Holt, Rinehart & Winston, 1960.

Jaspers, Karl. *Reason and Existenz.* New York, Noonday Press, 1955.

Koestler, Arthur. *Act of Creation.* London, Hutchinson & Co. Ltd., 1964.

Lévi-Strauss, Claude. *The Savage Mind.* University of Chicago Press, 1966.

Moore, Omar K., and Alan R. Anderson "The Structure of Personality," *The Review of Metaphysics,* XVI (1962), 212–36.

Tawney, R. H. *Religion and The Rise of Capitalism.* New York, New American Library, 1958.

Weber, Max. *The Protestant Ethic and The Spirit of Capitalism,* translated by Talcott Parsons. New York, Scribner, 1964.

# INDEX

Abron, 69, 100-27 *passim*
Adams, Robert, 156
Africa, 27, 73-74, 78-79, 128, 167;
  Australopithecinae fossils, 28-29,
  33, 36; *see also* Abron; Pygmies
*African Genesis, see* Ardrey, Robert
Aggression, 3, 19-24 *passim*, 40, 41,
  65, 77, 80, 99, 100, 121, 130-31,
  159, 163, 164, 165; and war, 3,
  53, 89, 127, 130, 131, 141, 144-
  45, 148, 163, 164 (*see also* War);
  Ardrey on, 25, 29, 30, 31, 33, 36,
  37, 38, 41-42, 62, 63, 76, 77, 79-
  80, 131, 144, 170; and hunting,
  distinction, 30, 122; Lorenz on,
  19, 28, 33, 36-45 *passim*, 49-54
  *passim*, 59, 60, 62, 126, 130, 131,
  144, 164, 170; primitive societies,
  30, 31, 121-22, 128-29, 130, 144;
  and ritualization, 36, 42-43, 44,
  130; Morris on, 84-85, 89; and
  morality, 163; and game playing, 164; *see also* Killing; Territoriality
Allen, Layman E., 88
Anagenesis, 4, 13, 14, 15, 18
Andrew, Richard, 35
Anthropology, 2, 51, 96-98, 101, 149-
  50, 151, 157; *see also* Social sciences
Ardrey, Robert, 1, 25-27, 28, 38-39,
  58, 72-73, 85, 165; *African Genesis,* 2, 26, 27, 33-34, 36, 38-39;
  *The Territorial Imperative,* 2, 26,
  27, 35, 41, 62, 65, 72, 73, 75, 79;
  on aggression, 25, 29, 30, 31, 33,
  36, 37, 38, 41-42, 62, 63, 76, 77,
  79-80, 131, 144, 170; on territoriality, 25-26, 33-34, 36, 37-38,
  62-70 *passim,* 72-80, 85, 126, 170;